Guide to Food Storage

Follow this guide for food storage, and you can be sure that what's in your freezer, refrigerator, and pantry is fresh-tasting and ready to use in recipes.

In the Freezer (at -10° to 0° F)

DAIRY

Cheese, hard	6 months
Cheese, soft	6 months
Egg substitute, unopened	1 year
Egg whites	1 year
Egg yolks	1 year
Ice cream, sherbet	1 month

FRUITS AND VEGETABLES

Commercially frozen fruits	1 year
Commercially frozen vegetables	8 to 12 months

MEATS, POULTRY, AND SEAFOOD

Beef, Lamb, Pork, and Veal

Chops, uncooked	4 to 6 months
Ground and stew meat, uncooked	3 to 4 months
Ham, fully cooked, half	1 to 2 months
Roasts, uncooked	4 to 12 months
Steaks, uncooked	6 to 12 months

Poultry

All cuts, cooked	4 months
Boneless or bone-in pieces, uncooked	9 months

Seafood

Fish, fatty, uncooked	2 to 3 months
Fish, lean, uncooked	6 months

In the Refrigerator (at 34° to 40° F)

DAIRY

Butter	1 to 3 months
Buttermilk	1 to 2 weeks
Cheese, hard, wedge, opened	6 months
Cheese, semihard, block, opened	3 to 4 weeks
Cream cheese, fat-free, light, and ⅓-less-fat	2 weeks
Egg substitute, opened	3 days
Fresh eggs in shell	3 to 5 weeks

MEATS, POULTRY, AND SEAFOOD

Beef, Lamb, Pork, and Veal

Ground and stew meat, uncooked	1 to 2 days
Roasts, uncooked	3 to 5 days
Steaks and chops, uncooked	3 to 5 days

Chicken, Turkey, and Seafood

All cuts, uncooked	1 to 2 days

FRUITS AND VEGETABLES

Apples, beets, cabbage, carrots, celery, citrus fruits, eggplant, and parsnips	2 to 3 weeks
Apricots, asparagus, berries, cauliflower, cucumbers, mushrooms, okra, peaches, pears, peas, peppers, plums, salad greens, and summer squash	2 to 4 days
Corn, husked	1 day

In the Pantry (keep these at room temperature for 6 to 12 months)

BAKING AND COOKING STAPLES

- Baking powder
- Biscuit and baking mixes
- Broth, canned
- Cooking spray
- Honey
- Mayonnaise, fat-free, low-fat, and light (unopened)
- Milk, canned evaporated fat-free
- Milk, nonfat dry powder
- Mustard, prepared (unopened)
- Oils, olive and vegetable
- Pasta, dried
- Peanut butter
- Rice, instant and regular
- Salad dressings, bottled (unopened)
- Seasoning sauces, bottled
- Tuna, canned

FRUITS, LEGUMES, AND VEGETABLES

- Fruits, canned
- Legumes (beans, lentils, peas), dried or canned
- Tomato products, canned
- Vegetables, canned

WeightWatchers®
our best
Quick
& Easy meals

Oxmoor House®

©2010 by Oxmoor House, Inc.
P.O. Box 360220, Des Moines, IA 50336-0220

ISBN-13: 978-0-8487-3357-5
ISBN-10: 0-8487-3357-6
Library of Congress Control Number: 2009937179
Printed in the United States of America
First printing 2010

Be sure to check with your health-care provider before making any changes in your diet.

Weight Watchers and **POINTS** are registered trademarks of Weight Watchers International, Inc., and are used under license by Oxmoor House, Inc.

Oxmoor House, Inc.

VP, Publishing Director: Jim Childs
Editorial Director: Susan Payne Dobbs
Brand Manager: Victoria Alfonso
Managing Editor: Laurie S. Herr
Senior Editor: Heather Averett

Weight Watchers® Our Best Quick & Easy Meals

Editor: Andrea C. Kirkland, M.S., R.D.
Project Editor: Emily Chappell
Senior Designer: Emily Albright Parrish
Director, Test Kitchens: Elizabeth Tyler Austin
Assistant Director, Test Kitchens: Julie Christopher
Test Kitchens Professionals: Allison E. Cox, Julie Gunter, Kathleen Royal Phillips,
    Catherine Crowell Steele, Ashley T. Strickland
Photography Director: Jim Bathie
Senior Photo Stylist: Kay E. Clarke
Associate Photo Stylist: Katherine Eckert Coyne
Production Manager: Theresa Beste-Farley

Contributors

Designer and Compositor: Carol O. Loria
Copy Editor: Dolores Hydock
Proofreader: Stacey Loyless
Indexer: Mary Ann Laurens
Interns: Ina Ables, Sarah Bellinger, Georgia Dodge, Perri K. Hubbard,
    Maggie McDaris, Allison Sperando
Food Stylist: Alyson Haynes, Ana Price Kelly, Iris O'Brien,
    Laura Zapalowski
Photographer: Lee Harrelson
Photo Stylists: Missy Neville Crawford, Mindi Shapiro

Cover: Chicken Mozzarella and Penne (page 105)

Contents

Introduction

Recipes

Cook Fast Eat Well

Preparing mouthwatering, hassle-free meals is now within reach—thanks to this all-new *Our Best Quick and Easy Meals* cookbook from Weight Watchers® Books. With this collection of 200 recipes, menus, step-by-step game plans, and **POINTS**® values, you'll be armed with a variety of ways to cook smarter, make the most of your precious time, and—best of all—ensure that your efforts deliver incredibly delightful dishes night after night.

Smart Strategies for the Quick Cook

Follow these tips for organizing your kitchen, planning meals, and grocery shopping and you'll be only minutes away from serving home-cooked meals any night of the week.

Get organized.

• Store commonly used ingredients and tools in the same place every time so you'll always be able to find them quickly and easily.

• Alphabetize spices and seasonings so they're quick to find. If you have room, dried seasonings store best in the freezer. If you store them in a cabinet, place them in a cool area away from heat or light.

• Store wooden spoons, rubber and metal spatulas, tongs, wire whisks, cooking spoons and forks, potato masher, kitchen shears, basting brush, and a ladle in large decorative containers or jars near your cooktop and mixing center. Store potholders close to the oven, cooktop, and microwave for quick access.

• Attach a magnetic shopping list to the refrigerator door for jotting down items to purchase as you think of them.

Plan ahead.

• Take time to plan meals around your schedule. Super-busy weeknights might call for a quick-to-assemble salad, a simple soup that requires only a few minutes of hands-on prep, or leftovers that just need to be reheated.

• Develop a repertoire of about 12 recipes your family loves. Bookmark them with sticky notes or keep copies in a binder.

• Think about how you will organize your time when cooking. Read recipes ahead of time and think about which steps can be done simultaneously. The more you plan in advance, the more quickly your meals will come together.

• Create a blank shopping list on your computer in categories that match the aisles in the grocery store. Categories might include: canned goods/convenience items; pasta/rice/grains; cleaning supplies/toiletries; deli/bakery foods; produce; meats; dairy; and frozen foods. Print several lists at a time to keep handy.

• Put your groceries through checkout in categories. Once you arrive home, you'll be able to put away items quickly because they'll already be sorted.
• Gather all of your ingredients and equipment before you start cooking. This will reduce the number of trips to your cabinets and refrigerator to dig for ingredients and tools at the last minute.

Stock up to shop less.
• Keep your pantry, fridge, and freezer well stocked with commonly used food items to avoid last-minute shopping trips for missing ingredients.
• Store a supply of basic, nonperishable items so you can improvise main- and side-dish recipes when needed.
• Take inventory of what you have on hand and make a list of the items you need to replace.

Take advantage of convenience items and prepared fresh ingredients at your supermarket.
• Save prep and cook time by using convenient potato products, such as refrigerated or frozen wedges, quarters, hash browns, and mashed potatoes. If you're using fresh potatoes, leave the skin on to save prep time and to preserve nutrients and fiber.

• Forgo coring, peeling, and slicing fresh fruit yourself. Look in the produce section for presliced apple; seeded or unseeded melon chunks; cored pineapple; and bottles of sliced fresh citrus sections, mango, and papaya.
• Keep bottled whole peeled garlic cloves on hand to add flavor to meats or side dishes.
• Simplify side dishes by using couscous, quick-cooking grits, precooked microwavable rice, and fresh pasta (it cooks more quickly than prepackaged dry).
• Eliminate chopping and slicing veggies by using packaged prechopped vegetables from the produce section of your supermarket, such as broccoli florets, shredded cabbage, angel hair slaw, carrots, celery, mixed stir-fry vegetables, and onion.
• Use baby spinach instead of regular fresh spinach so you won't have to trim stems or chop.
• Buy peeled and deveined shrimp. Ask someone in your seafood department to cook your shrimp while you finish your grocery shopping.
• Use one of the many precooked chicken products now available: rotisserie chicken, packaged preshredded or grilled chicken, or frozen chopped chicken.

About the Recipes

Weight Watchers® *Our Best Quick and Easy Meals* gives you the nutrition facts you need to stay on track. Every recipe in this book includes a **POINTS®** value. For more information on Weight Watchers, see page 5.

Each recipe has a list of nutrients—including calories, fat, percent of calories from fat, saturated fat, protein, carbohydrates, dietary fiber, cholesterol, iron, sodium, and calcium—as well as a serving size and the number of servings. This information makes it easy for you to use the recipes for any weight-loss program that you choose to follow. Measurements are abbreviated g (grams) and mg (milligrams). Nutritional values used in our calculations come from either The Food Processor, Version 8.9 (ESHA Research), or are provided by food manufacturers.

Numbers are based on these assumptions:
• Unless otherwise indicated, meat, poultry, and fish always refer to skinned, boned, and cooked servings.
• When we give a range for an ingredient (3 to 3½ cups flour, for instance), we calculate using the lesser amount.
• Some alcohol calories evaporate during heating; the analysis reflects this.
• Only the amount of marinade absorbed by the food is used in calculations.
• Garnishes and optional ingredients are not included in an analysis.

Safety Note: Cooking spray should never be used near direct heat. Always remove a pan from heat before spraying it with cooking spray.

A Note on Diabetic Exchanges: You may notice that the nutrient analysis for each recipe does not include Diabetic Exchanges. Most dietitians and diabetes educators are now teaching people with diabetes to count total carbohydrates at each meal and snack, rather than counting exchanges. Counting carbohydrates gives people with diabetes more flexibility in their food choices and seems to be an effective way to manage blood glucose.

POINTS values
The Momentum™ Program is based on the Weight Watchers **POINTS** Weight-Loss System and encourages you to focus on foods that will help you lose weight, feel fuller longer, and stay satisfied.
• Every food has a **POINTS** value that is based on calories, fat grams, and fiber grams in a specific portion of food.
• Members keep track of **POINTS** values and stick to their individual daily **POINTS** Target, which is the number of **POINTS** values a person needs to eat each day in order to lose weight.
• You can enjoy a full range of food options at home, on the go, or when dining out.

Breakfast

Menu
POINTS value
per serving: 4

Sweet-Spiced Berry
Breakfast Parfait

Game Plan

1. Quarter strawberries; grate orange rind.

2. Prepare fruit mixture.

3. Assemble parfaits.

Sweet-Spiced Berry Breakfast Parfaits

prep: 13 minutes   *POINTS* value: 4

Granola is widely thought of as a healthful snack or breakfast food, but be advised—a careful review of the label can reveal unwanted fat and sugar. We used a low-fat version to keep the calories in this parfait to a minimum.

  2   cups strawberries, quartered
  1   cup blueberries
  3   tablespoons "measures-like-sugar" calorie-free sweetener (such as Splenda)
1½ teaspoons grated fresh orange rind
  3   tablespoons fresh orange juice
  ½ teaspoon ground cinnamon
  4   (6-ounce) cartons vanilla fat-free yogurt
  1   cup low-fat granola (such as Back To Nature)

1. Combine first 6 ingredients in a medium bowl; toss well.
2. Spoon ½ carton yogurt (about ⅓ cup) into each of 4 (8-ounce) parfait glasses.
Top each with 2 tablespoons granola and about ⅓ cup fruit mixture. Repeat layers.
Yield: 4 servings (serving size: 1 parfait).

Per serving: CALORIES 211 (8% from fat); FAT 1.9g (saturated fat 0.3g); PROTEIN 8.9g; CARBOHYDRATES 48.1g; FIBER 4.6g; CHOLESTEROL 0mg; IRON 1.4mg; SODIUM 76mg; CALCIUM 179mg

Smoked Salmon Bagel Sandwiches

prep: 5 minutes • **cook:** 6 minutes

POINTS value: 5

Dress up a humble bagel with cream cheese by adding salty smoked salmon and protein-packed hard-cooked egg slices. Look for packages of precooked eggs alongside the raw eggs in the dairy case at your local supermarket.

- ¼ cup (2 ounces) tub-style light cream cheese with chives and onion
- 4 (3-inch) mini whole wheat bagels (such as Thomas'), split and toasted
- 2 ounces smoked salmon
- ¼ cup thinly sliced red onion
- 2 precooked, peeled eggs (such as Eggland's Best), sliced

1. Spread cream cheese evenly over each bagel half. Top bottom halves with salmon, onion, and sliced egg; top with remaining bagel halves. **Yield:** 4 servings (serving size: 1 sandwich).

Per serving: CALORIES 232 (33% from fat); FAT 8.6g (saturated fat 4.2g); PROTEIN 12.3g; CARBOHYDRATES 27.5g; FIBER 3.1g; CHOLESTEROL 108mg; IRON 1.7mg; SODIUM 597mg; CALCIUM 76mg

Summer Fruit Salad

prep: 8 minutes

POINTS value: 1

- 2 tablespoons powdered sugar
- 2 teaspoons fresh lemon juice
- 2 teaspoons orange juice
- 2½ cups thinly sliced peeled peaches
- 1 cup blueberries
- 1 cup raspberries

1. Combine first 3 ingredients in a large bowl, stirring with a whisk. Add peaches, blueberries, and raspberries; toss gently to coat. Serve immediately, or cover and chill until ready to serve. **Yield:** 4 servings (serving size: about 1 cup).

Per serving: CALORIES 97 (6% from fat); FAT 0.6g (saturated fat 0g); PROTEIN 1.5g; CARBOHYDRATES 23.1g; FIBER 4.3g; CHOLESTEROL 0mg; IRON 0.6mg; SODIUM 1mg; CALCIUM 16mg

Menu
POINTS value
per serving: 6

Smoked Salmon Bagel Sandwich

Summer Fruit Salad

Game Plan

1. Prepare fruit salad.

2. While bagels toast:
  • Slice onions and eggs.

3. Assemble sandwiches.

Menu
POINTS value
per serving: 4

Huevos Rancheros

Chili-Dusted Mango

Game Plan

1. Chop and measure cilantro; prepare Chili-Dusted Mango.

2. While tortillas cook:
  • Measure salsa and sour cream.

3. Cook eggs.

4. Assemble Huevos Rancheros.

Huevos Rancheros

prep: 2 minutes • **cook:** 8 minutes   *POINTS* value: 3

Traditionally served for breakfast, this spicy Mexican egg dish makes a delicious dinner, too. For more heat, use a hot or extra-hot fresh salsa.

    4 (5½-inch) corn tortillas
    Cooking spray
    4 large eggs
    ¼ teaspoon salt
    ¼ teaspoon black pepper
    ½ cup refrigerated fresh salsa
    ¼ cup reduced-fat sour cream
    1 tablespoon chopped fresh cilantro

1. Heat a large nonstick skillet over medium-high heat; coat tortillas with cooking spray. Add tortillas to pan, and cook 2 to 3 minutes on each side or until golden and crispy; set tortillas aside.

2. Coat pan with cooking spray. Crack eggs, 1 at a time, into pan; sprinkle evenly with salt and pepper. Cook eggs 2 to 3 minutes on each side or until desired degree of doneness.

3. Place 1 egg on each tortilla; top each with 2 tablespoons salsa, 1 tablespoon sour cream, and ¾ teaspoon cilantro. **Yield:** 4 servings (serving size: 1 topped tortilla).

Per serving: CALORIES 165 (36% from fat); FAT 6.6g (saturated fat 2.5g); PROTEIN 8.5g; CARBOHYDRATES 16.1g; FIBER 2.2g; CHOLESTEROL 188mg; IRON 1.7mg; SODIUM 344mg; CALCIUM 93mg

Chili-Dusted Mango

prep: 8 minutes   *POINTS* value: 1

    2 ripe mangoes, peeled, seeded, and cut into ½-inch slices
    2 teaspoons fresh lime juice
    ¼ teaspoon chili powder
    1 teaspoon chopped fresh cilantro

1. Arrange mango slices evenly on 4 plates; sprinkle evenly with lime juice, chili powder, and cilantro. **Yield:** 4 servings (serving size: ¼ of mango slices).

Per serving: CALORIES 72; FAT 0.3g (saturated fat 0.1g); PROTEIN 0.6g; CARBOHYDRATES 18.9g; FIBER 2g; CHOLESTEROL 0mg; IRON 0.2mg; SODIUM 7mg; CALCIUM 11mg

pictured on page 33

English Muffins Topped with Tomato-Chive Baked Eggs

prep: 6 minutes • **cook:** 13 minutes   *POINTS* value: 3

These eggs are easy enough to prepare on busy mornings, yet special enough to serve to guests at your next brunch.

Butter-flavored cooking spray
2   medium tomatoes, seeded and chopped
2   tablespoons minced fresh chives
4   large eggs
½   teaspoon salt
½   teaspoon freshly ground black pepper
2   whole wheat English muffins, halved and toasted

1. Preheat oven to 375°.
2. Coat 4 (4-ounce) ramekins or custard cups with cooking spray. Spoon tomato and chives evenly into ramekins. Break 1 egg on top of tomato mixture in each ramekin; sprinkle evenly with salt and pepper.
3. Bake at 375° for 13 minutes or until desired degree of doneness. Gently remove baked eggs from ramekins and place on top of cut sides of English muffins. **Yield:** 4 servings (serving size: 1 baked egg and 1 English muffin half).

Per serving: CALORIES 145 (37% from fat); FAT 6g (saturated fat 1.6g); PROTEIN 10g; CARBOHYDRATES 15.5g; FIBER 2.3g; CHOLESTEROL 212mg; IRON 1.9mg; SODIUM 483mg; CALCIUM 75mg

Menu
POINTS value
per serving: 3

English Muffin Topped with Tomato-Chive Baked Eggs

1 cup steamed asparagus spears
POINTS value: 0

Game Plan

1. Chop tomatoes and chives; prepare ramekins.

2. While eggs bake:
• Toast English muffins.
• Steam asparagus.

Menu
POINTS value
per serving: 5

Garden Scrambled Eggs

Garlic-Roasted Potatoes

Game Plan

1. While oven preheats:
   - Quarter potatoes; toss with oil and seasonings.

2. While potatoes cook:
   - Prepare eggs.

Garden Scrambled Eggs

prep: 5 minutes • **cook:** 5 minutes

POINTS value: 3

Bring garden freshness to your table with these veggie-laden scrambled eggs. Red tomato, juicy onion, and green bell pepper perk up this traditional breakfast dish.

Butter-flavored cooking spray
¾ cup refrigerated prechopped tomato, onion, and bell pepper mix
4 large eggs
4 large egg whites
2 tablespoons chopped fresh parsley
6 tablespoons reduced-fat sour cream
1 tablespoon Dijon mustard
Dash of salt
Dash of black pepper

1. Heat a large nonstick skillet over medium heat. Coat pan with cooking spray; add tomato mixture. Coat vegetables with cooking spray; cook 3 minutes or until vegetables are tender, stirring often.
2. While vegetables cook, combine eggs, egg whites, and next 5 ingredients in a medium bowl, stirring with a whisk.
3. Add egg mixture to pan; cook over medium heat 2 minutes. Do not stir until mixture begins to set on bottom. Draw a heat-resistant spatula through egg mixture to form large curds. Do not stir constantly. Egg mixture is done when thickened, but still moist. Serve immediately. **Yield:** 4 servings (serving size: ¼ of egg mixture).

Per serving: CALORIES 133 (54% from fat); FAT 8g (saturated fat 3.3g); PROTEIN 11g; CARBOHYDRATES 4.3g; FIBER 0.5g; CHOLESTEROL 220mg; IRON 1.2mg; SODIUM 263mg; CALCIUM 59mg

Garlic-Roasted Potatoes

prep: 5 minutes • **cook:** 15 minutes

POINTS value: 2

1 pound small red potatoes (about 8 potatoes), cut into quarters
1 teaspoon olive oil
¼ teaspoon salt
¼ teaspoon garlic powder
¼ teaspoon black pepper
Butter-flavored cooking spray

1. Preheat oven to 500°.
2. Place potatoes in a large bowl. Drizzle with oil; toss well. Sprinkle with salt, garlic powder, and pepper; toss until potatoes are evenly coated with spices. Arrange wedges in a single layer on a large rimmed baking sheet coated with cooking spray.
3. Bake at 500° for 15 minutes or until browned. **Yield:** 4 servings (serving size: ¾ cup).

Per serving: CALORIES 92 (15% from fat); FAT 2g (saturated fat 0.2g); PROTEIN 2.2g; CARBOHYDRATES 18.2g; FIBER 2g; CHOLESTEROL 0mg; IRON 0.8mg; SODIUM 152mg; CALCIUM 12mg

Asparagus, Ham, and Blue Cheese Frittata

prep: 2 minutes • **cook:** 16 minutes • **other:** 2 minutes   *POINTS* value: 3

This frittata, filled with crisp-tender asparagus, smoky ham, and creamy pockets of blue cheese, is a great way to kick off your work or weekend activities. For maximum blue cheese flavor, choose a potent variety, such as Maytag. For a heartier meal and an additional *POINTS* value of 1, serve with 1 cup of mixed melon.

  1   cup water
  8   ounces thin asparagus spears, trimmed and cut into 2-inch pieces
Butter-flavored cooking spray
  4   ounces thinly sliced reduced-sodium ham (such as Boar's Head), chopped
 ⅓   cup (about 1½ ounces) crumbled blue cheese
  5   tablespoons finely chopped green onions, divided
1¼ cups egg substitute
 ¼   teaspoon freshly ground black pepper

1. Bring 1 cup water to a boil in a 9-inch nonstick skillet over medium-high heat. Add asparagus; reduce heat, and simmer, uncovered, 3 minutes or just until crisp-tender. Remove asparagus from pan; drain well, and set aside.

2. Reduce heat to medium, and coat pan with cooking spray. Add ham to pan, and sauté 1 minute. Reduce heat to medium-low; sprinkle asparagus, blue cheese, and 3 tablespoons green onions over ham in pan. Pour egg substitute over ham mixture. Cover and cook 12 minutes. Uncover pan; gently lift edges of frittata with a rubber spatula, and tilt pan to allow any uncooked egg mixture to flow underneath. Sprinkle with remaining green onions. Remove from heat; cover and let stand 2 minutes.

3. Sprinkle frittata with pepper. Cut into 4 wedges, and serve immediately.

Yield: 4 servings (serving size: 1 wedge).

Per serving: CALORIES 153 (38% from fat); FAT 6.4g (saturated fat 2.5g); PROTEIN 18.2g; CARBOHYDRATES 4.9g; FIBER 1.6g; CHOLESTEROL 21mg; IRON 3.1mg; SODIUM 526mg; CALCIUM 117mg

---

Menu
POINTS value
per serving: 6

Asparagus, Ham, and Blue Cheese Frittata

1 (1-ounce) slice whole-grain toast with 1 teaspoon butter
POINTS value: 3

Game Plan

1. While asparagus steams:
- Chop ham and green onions.
- Measure blue cheese and egg substitute.

2. While egg mixture cooks:
- Toast bread.

Menu
POINTS value
per serving: 5

Feta and Spinach Omelet

1 cup precubed cantaloupe
POINTS value: 1

Game Plan

1. Chop onion and spinach.

2. While onion cooks:
  • Blend eggs and cheese.

3. Cook omelet.

Feta and Spinach Omelet

prep: 2 minutes • **cook:** 10 minutes   **POINTS** value: 4

Blending the feta cheese with the eggs ensures that the cheese flavor is evenly dispersed throughout the omelet.

> Olive oil–flavored cooking spray
> 1   cup chopped onion
> 2   cups chopped fresh baby spinach
> ¼   teaspoon salt
> ¼   teaspoon freshly ground black pepper
> 2   large eggs
> 3   large egg whites
> ⅓   cup (about 1½ ounces) crumbled reduced-fat feta cheese

1. Heat a 9- to 10-inch nonstick skillet over medium heat. Coat pan with cooking spray. Add onion; coat onion with cooking spray, and cook 5 minutes, stirring occasionally. Add spinach, salt, and pepper; cook 1 minute or just until spinach wilts. Remove spinach mixture from pan; set aside, and keep warm. Wipe pan with paper towels, and place over medium heat. Recoat pan with cooking spray.
2. Place eggs, egg whites, and cheese in a blender; process until smooth.
3. Pour egg mixture into pan, and cook over medium heat. Do not stir until a layer of egg has set on bottom of pan. Gently lift edges of omelet with a rubber spatula, and tilt pan to allow any uncooked egg mixture to flow underneath. Continue until top of omelet is almost set; remove pan from heat.
4. Spoon spinach mixture over half of omelet; fold omelet in half. Cut omelet in half, and serve immediately. **Yield:** 2 servings (serving size: ½ omelet).

Per serving: CALORIES 178 (40% from fat); FAT 7.9g (saturated fat 3.4g); PROTEIN 17.7g; CARBOHYDRATES 10.3g; FIBER 2.5g; CHOLESTEROL 218mg; IRON 2mg; SODIUM 756mg; CALCIUM 140mg

Sausage-Avocado Breakfast Tacos

prep: 6 minutes • **cook:** 7 minutes   *POINTS* value: 6

In our version of this Texas favorite, we've substituted lean turkey sausage for pork sausage and a whole wheat tortilla for the traditional flour tortilla. The result rivals the original but has a lower *POINTS* value.

Cooking spray
2 uncooked turkey sausage breakfast links (about 2¼ ounces; such as Jennie-O)
⅓ cup prechopped onion
4 large eggs
4 large egg whites
½ teaspoon hot sauce
¼ teaspoon salt
½ medium avocado, diced
4 (6-inch) whole wheat tortillas (such as Mission)
¼ cup (1 ounce) preshredded reduced-fat 4-cheese Mexican blend cheese
½ cup fresh salsa

1. Heat a large nonstick skillet over medium heat. Coat pan with cooking spray.

2. Remove casings from sausage. Add sausage and onion to pan; cook 5 minutes or until sausage is browned, stirring to crumble sausage.

3. Combine eggs, egg whites, hot sauce, and salt, stirring with a whisk. Add egg mixture to sausage mixture. Cook 2 minutes over medium-high heat, stirring slowly and frequently. Remove from heat. Gently toss in avocado.

4. Warm tortillas in microwave according to package directions. Spoon filling evenly down the center of each tortilla. Sprinkle each taco with 1 tablespoon cheese; fold in half. Top each taco with 2 tablespoons fresh salsa. **Yield:** 4 servings (serving size: 1 taco).

Per serving: CALORIES 280 (44% from fat); FAT 13.8g (saturated fat 3.3g); PROTEIN 17.8g; CARBOHYDRATES 17.8g; FIBER 9.5g; CHOLESTEROL 194mg; IRON 1.8mg; SODIUM 729mg; CALCIUM 130mg

---

Menu
POINTS value
per serving: 7

Sausage-Avocado Breakfast Taco

1 orange
POINTS value: 1

Game Plan

1. While sausage cooks:
• Combine eggs with hot sauce and salt.
• Dice avocado.

2. While eggs cook:
• Warm tortillas.

3. Assemble tacos.

Menu
POINTS value
per serving: 6

**Turkey-Sausage
Breakfast Bowl**

**1 cup strawberries
POINTS** value: 1

Game Plan

1. While potatoes cook:
- Prepare sausage and grits.
- Measure Cheddar cheese and egg substitute.
- Cook eggs.

2. Microwave potato mixture.

Turkey-Sausage Breakfast Bowl

prep: 4 minutes • **cook:** 11 minutes   **POINTS** value: 5

This filling meal for two features cheesy grits, potatoes, egg substitute, and sausage—all with a fraction of the fat and calories you'd find in a frozen-food breakfast bowl.

½   cup refrigerated diced potatoes with onion (such as Simply Potatoes)
     Cooking spray
1   fully cooked turkey sausage patty
3   tablespoons quick-cooking grits
¾   cup water
¼   teaspoon salt
¼   cup (1 ounce) reduced-fat shredded sharp Cheddar cheese, divided
½   cup egg substitute
⅛   teaspoon black pepper

1. Heat a small nonstick skillet over medium-high heat; coat potatoes with cooking spray, and add to pan. Cover and cook 8 minutes or until potatoes are lightly browned, stirring occasionally.
2. While potatoes cook, heat sausage patty in microwave according to package directions. Crumble sausage patty, and set aside. Combine grits, water, and salt in a microwave-safe bowl. Microwave at HIGH 2 to 3 minutes or until thick, stirring after 1 minute. Remove from microwave; stir in 2 tablespoons cheese.
3. Combine egg substitute and pepper; add to pan with cooked potatoes, and reduce heat to low. Cook until eggs are just set, stirring occasionally. Spoon potato mixture over grits; top with crumbled sausage, and sprinkle with remaining 2 tablespoons cheese. Cover bowl with wax paper; microwave at HIGH 15 seconds or until cheese melts. Serve immediately. **Yield:** 2 servings (serving size: about ¾ cup).

Per serving: CALORIES 227 (31% from fat); FAT 7.7g (saturated fat 3.3g); PROTEIN 18.6g; CARBOHYDRATES 19.1g; FIBER 0.6g; CHOLESTEROL 40mg; IRON 2.5mg; SODIUM 796mg; CALCIUM 142mg

Ham-Smothered Cheese Grits

prep: 4 minutes • **cook:** 13 minutes

POINTS value: 5

Add a little bit of warm water to the grits before serving if they become too thick.

2⅔   cups water
⅔   cup uncooked quick-cooking grits
1   cup (4 ounces) reduced-fat shredded sharp Cheddar cheese
¼   teaspoon salt
¼   teaspoon freshly ground black pepper
Cooking spray
1   small poblano chile, seeded and finely chopped
½   cup finely chopped onion
4   ounces prechopped lean ham (about 1 cup)
¼   cup water

1. Bring 2⅔ cups water to a boil in a medium saucepan. Reduce heat to medium-low, and slowly add grits, stirring constantly with a whisk. Cover and cook 7 minutes or until thick, stirring frequently. Remove from heat; add cheese, salt, and black pepper, stirring until cheese melts.
2. While grits cook, heat a large nonstick skillet over medium-high heat until hot. Coat pan with cooking spray. Add poblano chile and onion; cook 4 minutes or just until onion is tender, stirring frequently. Add ham and ¼ cup water; cook just until thoroughly heated.
3. Spoon grits evenly onto 4 plates; spoon ¼ cup ham mixture in center of grits.
Yield: 4 servings (serving size: ⅔ cup grits and ¼ cup ham mixture).

Per serving: CALORIES 224 (29% from fat); FAT 7.2g (saturated fat 3.9g); PROTEIN 15.2g; CARBOHYDRATES 24.6g; FIBER 1.3g; CHOLESTEROL 29mg; IRON 1.2mg; SODIUM 665mg; CALCIUM 265mg

Menu
POINTS value
per serving: 6

Ham-Smothered Cheese Grits

½ cup orange juice
POINTS value: 1

Game Plan

1. While water for grits comes to a boil:
• Chop chile and onion.
• Measure ham.

2. While grits simmer:
• Measure cheese.
• Cook chile, onion, and ham.

Menu

POINTS value
per serving: 5

Mini Breakfast Pizza

Citrus-Peach Salad

Game Plan

1. While oven preheats:
- Prepare biscuit dough on baking sheet.
- Chop ham and bell pepper; measure ingredients.

2. While pizzas bake:
- Prepare salad.

Mini Breakfast Pizzas

prep: 5 minutes • **cook:** 13 minutes

POINTS value: 3

Double the recipe and use the whole can of biscuits to make 10 individual pizzas.

  1   (7.5-ounce) can refrigerated biscuit dough (such as Pillsbury)
Cooking spray
⅔   cup egg substitute
⅛   cup (1 ounce) diced deli ham
⅓   cup chopped red bell pepper
⅔   cup reduced-fat shredded sharp Cheddar cheese

1. Preheat oven to 350°.
2. Place dough for 5 biscuits on a baking sheet coated with cooking spray; reserve remaining dough for another use. Press dough into 5 (3- to 4-inch) rounds. Bake at 350° for 8 to 10 minutes or until golden.
3. While dough bakes, cook egg substitute according to package directions.
4. Remove baking sheet from oven; flatten crusts with a spatula. Top each crust evenly with egg, ham, bell pepper, and cheese. Bake an additional 5 minutes or until cheese melts. **Yield:** 5 servings (serving size: 1 pizza).

Per serving: CALORIES 128 (29% from fat); FAT 4.1g (saturated fat 2.2g); PROTEIN 9.6g; CARBOHYDRATES 12g; FIBER 0.5g; CHOLESTEROL 14mg; IRON 1.2mg; SODIUM 426mg; CALCIUM 120mg

Citrus-Peach Salad

prep: 10 minutes

POINTS value: 2

  1   cup diced peeled peaches (about 1 large)
¾   cup grapefruit sections (about 1 large)
½   cup orange sections (about 1 medium)
¼   cup orange juice
  2   teaspoons sugar
  1   tablespoon thinly sliced fresh basil

1. Combine first 3 ingredients in a medium bowl.
2. Microwave orange juice at HIGH 15 seconds. Stir in sugar. Pour orange juice mixture over fruit; stir in basil. **Yield:** 5 servings (serving size: about ½ cup).

Per serving: CALORIES 139 (29% from fat); FAT 0.2g (saturated fat 0g); PROTEIN 1.1g; CARBOHYDRATES 14.4g; FIBER 1.9g; CHOLESTEROL 0mg; IRON 0.2mg; SODIUM 1mg; CALCIUM 23mg

pictured on page 34

Monte Cristo Sandwiches

prep: 3 minutes • **cook:** 8 minutes

POINTS value: 7

Dip the sandwiches in the egg mixture for about 5 seconds on each side in order to use all the mixture. If you don't have a family-size griddle that will hold 4 sandwiches at once, you can use a large nonstick skillet and cook the sandwiches in two batches—the cook time will increase by about 6 minutes.

8 (1-ounce) slices cinnamon-raisin bread (such as Pepperidge Farm), toasted
4 (⅝-ounce) slices reduced-fat Swiss cheese (such as Alpine Lace)
6 ounces shaved deli ham (such as Oscar Mayer)
2 large eggs
6 tablespoons 1% low-fat milk
Cooking spray
2 teaspoons powdered sugar
¼ cup cranberry chutney (such as Crosse & Blackwell)

1. Top each of 4 bread slices with 1 cheese slice. Divide ham evenly over cheese; top with remaining bread slices.

2. Combine eggs and milk in a shallow dish, stirring well with a whisk.

3. Heat a large nonstick griddle over medium heat. Coat pan with cooking spray. Dip each sandwich in egg mixture, allowing excess to drip off. Add sandwiches to pan; cook 3 minutes on each side or until golden. Cut sandwiches diagonally in half, if desired; sprinkle with powdered sugar. Serve sandwiches with chutney.

Yield: 4 servings (serving size: 1 sandwich and 1 tablespoon chutney).

Per serving: CALORIES 309 (30% from fat); FAT 10.4g (saturated fat 3.4g); PROTEIN 20g; CARBOHYDRATES 34.6g; FIBER 0g; CHOLESTEROL 127mg; IRON 2.2mg; SODIUM 803mg; CALCIUM 195mg

---

Menu
POINTS value
per serving: 7

Monte Cristo Sandwich

Black Coffee
POINTS value: 0

Game Plan

1. While coffee brews:
• Measure ingredients and crack eggs.

2. Assemble sandwiches.

3. Cook sandwiches.

pictured on page 35

Waffles with Berry Syrup

prep: 3 minutes • **cook:** 2 minutes

POINTS value: 2

With fresh berries and store-bought frozen waffles made with whole grains, this recipe is both convenient and healthy. Look for frozen waffles in the freezer case alongside the other breads and pastries.

6 frozen low-fat multigrain waffles (such as Kashi)
1 cup sliced strawberries
½ cup blueberries
½ cup raspberries
½ cup sugar-free maple-flavored syrup (such as Mrs. Butterworth's)
1 tablespoon powdered sugar

1. Preheat oven to 350°.
2. Place waffles on a large baking sheet. Bake at 350° for 2 to 3 minutes or until warm and crisp.
3. While waffles bake, combine berries and syrup in a 2-cup glass measure. Microwave at HIGH 1 minute or just until warm.
4. Sift powdered sugar evenly over waffles, and serve with syrup. **Yield:** 6 servings (serving size: 1 waffle, about ½ teaspoon powdered sugar, and about ¼ cup syrup).

Per serving: CALORIES 123 (12% from fat); FAT 1.7g (saturated fat 0g); PROTEIN 4.4g; CARBOHYDRATES 26.9g; FIBER 4.5g; CHOLESTEROL 0mg; IRON 0.9mg; SODIUM 199mg; CALCIUM 38mg

Menu
POINTS value
per serving: 4

Waffle with Berry Syrup

2 slices cooked
reduced-fat bacon
POINTS value: 2

Game Plan

1. While oven preheats:
• Measure berries and syrup.
• Cook bacon.

2. While waffles bake:
• Prepare syrup.

Hot Bulgur Cereal and Fruit

prep: 1 minute • **cook:** 12 minutes   *POINTS* value: 5

The delicately spiced, chewy texture of this tummy-warming cereal will satisfy even the most ravenous of appetites on a crisp fall morning.

3   cups 1% low-fat milk
1   cup uncooked bulgur
¼   teaspoon salt
½   teaspoon ground cinnamon
2   tablespoons brown sugar blend (such as Splenda)
½   cup dried mixed fruit bits (such as Sun-Maid)

1. Bring first 3 ingredients to a boil in a medium saucepan over medium heat, stirring constantly. Reduce heat; cover and simmer milk mixture 7 minutes or until thick, stirring occasionally.

2. Remove pan from heat; stir in cinnamon and brown sugar blend. Add fruit, and stir; serve immediately. **Yield:** 4 servings (serving size: about 1 cup).

Per serving: CALORIES 261 (8% from fat); FAT 2.2g (saturated fat 1.2g); PROTEIN 11g; CARBOHYDRATES 50.7g; FIBER 7.6g; CHOLESTEROL 9mg; IRON 1.5mg; SODIUM 262mg; CALCIUM 243mg

Menu
POINTS value
per serving: 7

Hot Bulgur Cereal and Fruit

1 cup fat-free milk
POINTS value: 2

Game Plan

1. While milk mixture simmers:
 • Measure cinnamon, sugar blend, and dried fruit.

2. Stir cinnamon mixture into cooked bulgur.

3. Pour milk into glasses.

Menu
POINTS value
per serving: 7

Cranberry-Walnut Oatmeal

Game Plan

1. While milk mixture simmers:
- Toast walnuts.
- Measure quick-cooking oats and cranberries.

Cranberry-Walnut Oatmeal

prep: 3 minutes • **cook:** 14 minutes   ***POINTS*** value: 7

This warm, creamy, fiber-rich dish is a nourishing way to start any day. If you prefer a smaller portion, a ½-cup serving has a *POINTS* value of 3.

3½	cups fat-free milk
¼	cup firmly packed light brown sugar
½	teaspoon salt
2	cups quick-cooking oats
½	cup dried cranberries
¼	cup chopped walnuts, toasted

1. Combine first 3 ingredients in a medium saucepan; cook over medium heat 10 minutes or until bubbles form around edge. Stir in oats; cook 4 minutes or until thick, stirring occasionally. Stir in cranberries and walnuts. Serve immediately.
Yield: 4 servings (serving size: 1 cup).

Per serving: CALORIES 375 (18% from fat); FAT 7.7g (saturated fat 1g); PROTEIN 14.8g; CARBOHYDRATES 64.7g; FIBER 5.3g; CHOLESTEROL 4mg; IRON 2.3mg; SODIUM 393mg; CALCIUM 309mg

Fish & Shellfish

Pecan-Crusted
Barbecue Catfish

Sweet and Tangy
Mustard Coleslaw

Game Plan

1. While oven preheats:
   • Prepare panko mixture;
     dredge fish.

2. While fish cooks:
   • Prepare slaw.

Pecan-Crusted Barbecue Catfish

prep: 7 minutes • **cook:** 18 minutes   *POINTS* value: 6

Preheating the pan before adding the fish ensures that the fish will be crispy on both sides.

¾   cup panko (Japanese breadcrumbs)
⅓   cup finely chopped pecans
4   (6-ounce) farm-raised catfish fillets
½   teaspoon salt
3   tablespoons thick-and-spicy barbecue sauce (such as Kraft)
Cooking spray

1. Preheat oven to 425°. Place a large baking sheet in oven while preheating.
2. Combine panko and pecans in a shallow dish. Sprinkle fish with salt; brush both sides with barbecue sauce. Dredge fish in panko mixture. Remove pan from oven; coat pan with cooking spray. Coat fish with cooking spray, and place on pan. Bake at 425° for 18 minutes or until fish flakes easily when tested with a fork or until desired degree of doneness. **Yield:** 4 servings (serving size: 1 fillet).

Per serving: CALORIES 282 (35% from fat); FAT 10.9g (saturated fat 1.8g); PROTEIN 29.6g; CARBOHYDRATES 14.9g; FIBER 0.9g; CHOLESTEROL 99mg; IRON 1.3mg; SODIUM 542mg; CALCIUM 31mg

Sweet and Tangy Mustard Coleslaw

prep: 5 minutes   *POINTS* value: 2

2   tablespoons sugar
1   tablespoon canola oil
1   tablespoon cider vinegar
1   tablespoon prepared mustard
¼   teaspoon salt
4   cups packaged cabbage-and-carrot coleslaw
½   cup refrigerated prechopped tricolor bell pepper

1. Combine first 5 ingredients in a large bowl; stir well with a whisk. Add coleslaw and bell pepper; toss gently to coat. **Yield:** 4 servings (serving size: 1 cup).

Per serving: CALORIES 75 (44% from fat); FAT 4g (saturated fat 0.3g); PROTEIN 0.8g; CARBOHYDRATES 9.9g; FIBER 1.4g; CHOLESTEROL 0mg; IRON 0.3mg; SODIUM 196mg; CALCIUM 24mg

Broiled Cod with Almond Brown Butter

prep: 5 minutes • **cook:** 10 minutes   ***POINTS* value: 5**

  4   (6-ounce) cod fillets
  ½   teaspoon salt
  ⅛   teaspoon freshly ground black pepper
Cooking spray
  2   tablespoons butter
  ¼   cup sliced almonds
  ½   teaspoon grated lemon rind
  2   tablespoons fresh lemon juice

1. Preheat broiler.
2. Sprinkle fish with salt and pepper; arrange on a broiler pan coated with cooking spray. Broil 8 minutes or until fish flakes easily when tested with a fork or until desired degree of doneness.
3. While fish cooks, melt butter in a large nonstick skillet over medium heat; add almonds, and cook, stirring constantly, 1 to 2 minutes or until butter is lightly browned and almonds are toasted. Remove from heat; stir in lemon rind and juice. Spoon browned butter mixture evenly over fillets. **Yield:** 4 servings (serving size: 1 fillet and about 1 tablespoon browned butter mixture).

Per serving: CALORIES 226 (40% from fat); FAT 9.8g (sat 4.1g); PROTEIN 31.7g; CARBOHYDRATES 1.9g; FIBER 0.8g; CHOLESTEROL 88mg; IRON 0.9mg; SODIUM 423mg; CALCIUM 45mg

Skillet Asparagus and Roasted Bell Peppers

prep: 2 minutes • **cook:** 6 minutes   ***POINTS* value: 1**

Cooking spray
  3   tablespoons light balsamic vinaigrette, divided
  1   tablespoon water
 12   ounces asparagus spears, trimmed
  1   cup chopped bottled roasted red bell peppers
  2   tablespoons finely chopped fresh parsley

1. Heat a large nonstick skillet over medium-high heat. Coat pan with cooking spray. Add 1 tablespoon vinaigrette and 1 tablespoon water to pan. Place asparagus in pan. Cook, covered, 5 minutes or until asparagus is crisp-tender, stirring frequently. Remove from pan onto a serving platter.
2. Add 1 tablespoon vinaigrette to pan. Add bell pepper; cook 1 minute. Spoon over asparagus. Drizzle 1 tablespoon vinaigrette over asparagus and bell pepper; sprinkle with parsley. **Yield:** 4 servings (serving size: about 7 asparagus spears and ¼ cup bell pepper).

Per serving: CALORIES 37 (39% from fat); FAT 2g (saturated fat 0.2g); PROTEIN 1.2g; CARBOHYDRATES 4.1g; FIBER 1.2g; CHOLESTEROL 0mg; IRON 1.3mg; SODIUM 279mg; CALCIUM 16mg

---

Menu
***POINTS* value**
per serving: 6

Broiled Cod with Almond Brown Butter

Skillet Asparagus and Roasted Bell Peppers

Game Plan

1. While broiler preheats:
 • Trim asparagus, and chop bell peppers and parsley.
 • Grate lemon rind.
 • Assemble fish on pan.

2. While fish cooks:
 • Cook asparagus.
 • Prepare butter mixture.

pictured on page 36

Flounder with Warm Olive Salsa

prep: 3 minutes • **cook:** 7 minutes

POINTS value: 5

Squeezing a lemon wedge over the fish before drizzling with olive oil ties together the components of this dish.

Menu
POINTS value
per serving: 8

**Flounder with
Warm Olive Salsa**

**Lemon Couscous with
Toasted Pine Nuts**

Game Plan

1. While water for couscous comes to a boil:
   • Toast pine nuts, and measure couscous.

2. While couscous stands:
   • Chop tomatoes, olives, parsley, and oregano for salsa.
   • Season flounder.
   • Grate lemon rind.

3. Cook Warm Olive Salsa.

4. While fish cooks:
   • Toss couscous.

Cooking spray
   1   cup chopped plum tomato (about ⅓ pound)
  12   small pimiento-stuffed olives, chopped
   2   tablespoons chopped fresh parsley
  1½   teaspoons chopped fresh oregano, divided
   4   (6-ounce) flounder fillets, rinsed and patted dry
   ¼   teaspoon salt
   ¼   teaspoon freshly ground black pepper
   4   lemon wedges
   1   tablespoon extra-virgin olive oil

1. Heat a large nonstick skillet over medium-high heat. Coat pan with cooking spray. Add tomato; cook 1 minute or until thoroughly heated. Combine cooked tomato, olives, parsley, and ¾ teaspoon oregano in a small bowl; keep salsa warm.
2. Wipe pan dry with a paper towel; return pan to medium-high heat. Recoat pan with cooking spray. Sprinkle fish evenly with ¾ teaspoon oregano, salt, and pepper. Add fish to pan; cook 3 minutes on each side or until fish flakes easily when tested with a fork or until desired degree of doneness. Squeeze 1 lemon wedge over each fillet; drizzle evenly with oil. Top evenly with olive salsa.
Yield: 4 servings (serving size: 1 fillet and ¼ cup olive salsa).

Per serving: CALORIES 218 (32% from fat); FAT 8g (saturated fat 1.7g); PROTEIN 34.8g; CARBOHYDRATES 3.1g; FIBER 1g; CHOLESTEROL 85mg; IRON 1.4mg; SODIUM 485mg; CALCIUM 36mg

Lemon Couscous with Toasted Pine Nuts

prep: 3 minutes • **cook:** 5 minutes • **other:** 5 minutes

POINTS value: 3

   1   cup water
   ⅔   cup uncooked whole wheat couscous
   1   teaspoon grated lemon rind
   ¼   cup pine nuts, toasted
   2   teaspoons extra-virgin olive oil
   ¼   teaspoon salt

1. Bring 1 cup water to a boil in a small saucepan. Stir in couscous and lemon rind. Remove from heat; cover and let stand 5 minutes. Add pine nuts and remaining ingredients; fluff with a fork. **Yield:** 4 servings (serving size: about ½ cup).

Per serving: CALORIES 148 (52% from fat); FAT 8g (saturated fat 0.7g); PROTEIN 3.8g; CARBOHYDRATES 16.2g; FIBER 2.7g; CHOLESTEROL 0mg; IRON 1.1mg; SODIUM 146mg; CALCIUM 9mg

Orange Roughy with Sweet and Sour Glaze

prep: 5 minutes • **cook:** 7 minutes

POINTS value: 5

Orange roughy's subtle flavor makes it a terrific host for the sweet and salty, Asian-inspired sauce made of honey, lime, soy, and ginger.

2½ tablespoons honey
2   tablespoons fresh lime juice
1½ tablespoons less-sodium soy sauce
1   teaspoon grated peeled fresh ginger
1   teaspoon minced garlic
1   tablespoon olive oil, divided
4   (6-ounce) orange roughy fillets (about 1 inch thick)
¼   teaspoon salt
¼   teaspoon freshly ground black pepper
2   tablespoons sliced green onions

1. Combine first 5 ingredients and 1 teaspoon oil in a shallow dish, stirring with a whisk.
2. Sprinkle fish with salt and pepper. Place fish in marinade, turning to coat.
3. Heat a large nonstick skillet over medium-high heat until hot. Add remaining 2 teaspoons oil to hot pan. Cook fish in pan 3 minutes on each side or until fish flakes easily when tested with a fork or until desired degree of doneness. Reserve marinade. Remove fish from pan, and arrange on a serving platter.
4. Pour remaining marinade into hot pan. Cook over medium-high heat 1 minute or until slightly thick; pour over fish. Sprinkle with green onions. **Yield:** 4 servings (serving size: 1 fillet and 1 tablespoon glaze).

Per serving: CALORIES 208 (20% from fat); FAT 4.6g (saturated fat 0.5g); PROTEIN 28.4g; CARBOHYDRATES 12.5g; FIBER 0.2g; CHOLESTEROL 102mg; IRON 1.9mg; SODIUM 499mg; CALCIUM 22mg

Spicy-Sweet Broccoli

prep: 3 minutes • **cook:** 4 minutes

POINTS value: 1

1   (12-ounce) package refrigerated broccoli florets
2   tablespoons less-sodium soy sauce
2   tablespoons rice vinegar
1   tablespoon dark sesame oil
2   teaspoons sugar
¼   teaspoon crushed red pepper

1. Microwave broccoli according to package directions. Drain. Combine soy sauce and next 4 ingredients in a small bowl. Drizzle over cooked broccoli. **Yield:** 4 servings (serving size: ¾ cup).

Per serving: CALORIES 62 (55% from fat); FAT 4g (saturated fat 0.6g); PROTEIN 2.6g; CARBOHYDRATES 6.6g; FIBER 2.5g; CHOLESTEROL 0mg; IRON 0.8mg; SODIUM 473mg; CALCIUM 41mg

Menu
POINTS value
per serving: 8

Orange Roughy with Sweet and Sour Glaze

Spicy-Sweet Broccoli

½ cup precooked Basmati rice
POINTS value: 2

Game Plan

1. While broccoli cooks:
• Prepare marinade for fish.

2. While fish cooks:
• Toss broccoli with soy sauce mixture.
• Microwave rice.

Menu

POINTS value
per serving: 8

**Honey Mustard–Glazed
Salmon**

Lemony Green Beans Amandine

Game Plan

1. While broiler preheats:
  • Prepare glaze for fish.

2. While fish cooks:
  • Prepare green beans.

Honey Mustard–Glazed Salmon

prep: 5 minutes • **cook:** 10 minutes   *POINTS* value: 7

The basting sauce is a little sticky, so line the drip pan of your broiler pan with foil to make cleanup easy.

  2   tablespoons honey
  2   teaspoons Dijon mustard
  ¼   teaspoon salt
  ¼   teaspoon ground red pepper
  1   garlic clove, pressed
  4   (6-ounce) salmon fillets (about 1 inch thick)
  Cooking spray

1. Prepare broiler.
2. Combine first 5 ingredients in a small bowl, stirring with a whisk.
3. Place fish, skin side down, on a broiler pan coated with cooking spray. Brush fish with honey mixture. Broil fish 10 minutes or until fish flakes easily when tested with a fork or until desired degree of doneness. **Yield:** 4 servings (serving size: 1 fillet).

Per serving: CALORIES 308 (38% from fat); FAT 13.1g (saturated fat 3.1g); PROTEIN 36.3g; CARBOHYDRATES 9.5g; FIBER 0.1g; CHOLESTEROL 87mg; IRON 0.7mg; SODIUM 286mg; CALCIUM 23mg

Lemony Green Beans Amandine

prep: 2 minutes • **cook:** 4 minutes • **other:** 1 minute   *POINTS* value: 1

  1   (12-ounce) package pretrimmed green beans
  1   tablespoon butter
  2   tablespoons sliced almonds
  2   tablespoons fresh lemon juice
  ¼   teaspoon salt
  ⅛   teaspoon black pepper

1. Pierce green bean bag with a fork; microwave at HIGH 4 to 5 minutes or until tender. Let stand 1 minute.
2. While green beans cook, melt butter in a medium nonstick skillet over medium heat; add almonds. Cook 1 to 2 minutes or until almonds are lightly browned. Add beans and lemon juice to butter mixture in pan; toss gently. Sprinkle with salt and pepper. **Yield:** 4 servings (serving size: ¾ cup).

Per serving: CALORIES 71 (57% from fat); FAT 4.5g (saturated fat 1.9g); PROTEIN 2.3g; CARBOHYDRATES 7.4g; FIBER 3.3g; CHOLESTEROL 8mg; IRON 1mg; SODIUM 171mg; CALCIUM 41mg

pictured on page 37

Seared Salmon Fillets with Edamame Succotash

prep: 1 minute • **cook:** 14 minutes   ***POINTS*** value: 7

Applewood-smoked bacon imbues this upscale succotash with its sweet, smoky essence. Green soybeans replace the traditional limas. Fresh soybeans (edamame) are packed with potential health benefits. Each ½-cup serving contains 4 grams of fiber and only 3 grams of fat, all of which are the heart-healthy mono- and polyunsaturated kind. The beans are also high in soy protein, which may help reduce cholesterol when part of a low-fat diet.

3	applewood-smoked bacon slices
4	(6-ounce) salmon fillets (about 1 inch thick)
¼	teaspoon salt
¼	teaspoon freshly ground black pepper
¼	cup water
1	(8-ounce) container refrigerated prechopped tomato, onion, and bell pepper mix
1	cup frozen yellow and white whole-kernel corn
1	cup frozen shelled edamame (green soybeans)
½	teaspoon dried thyme
⅛	teaspoon salt

1. Cook bacon in a large nonstick skillet over medium heat 7 minutes or until crisp.
2. While bacon cooks, sprinkle fish evenly with ¼ teaspoon salt and black pepper. When bacon is done, transfer it to paper towels to drain; crumble bacon.
3. Add fish, skin side up, to drippings in pan. Cook 4 minutes over medium-high heat or until browned. Turn fish over; add crumbled bacon, ¼ cup water, and remaining ingredients to pan. Cover and steam 3 minutes or until fish flakes easily when tested with a fork or until desired degree of doneness. Serve fish over succotash. **Yield:** 4 servings (serving size: 1 fillet and about ¾ cup succotash).

Per serving: CALORIES 339 (32% from fat); FAT 12g (saturated fat 2.6g); PROTEIN 44.1g; CARBOHYDRATES 13.7g; FIBER 3.2g; CHOLESTEROL 105mg; IRON 2.5mg; SODIUM 512mg; CALCIUM 53mg

---

Menu
POINTS value
per serving: 7

Seared Salmon Fillets with Edamame Succotash

Game Plan

1. While bacon cooks:
  • Season fish.
  • Measure prechopped tomato mixture, corn, and edamame.

2. Prepare fish and succotash.

Menu
POINTS value
per serving: 8

**Broiled Swordfish with
Simple Puttanesca Sauce**

**Sautéed Zucchini
and Bell Peppers**

**½ cup angel hair pasta
POINTS value: 2**

Game Plan

1. While broiler preheats and water for pasta comes to a boil:
   • Prepare vegetables for side dish and sauce. Chop olives and capers.
   • Assemble fish on pan.
2. While fish cooks:
   • Cook sauce.
   • Cook pasta.
3. While fish and sauce cook:
   • Sauté vegetables for side dish.

Broiled Swordfish with Simple Puttanesca Sauce

prep: 4 minutes • **cook:** 15 minutes   *POINTS* value: 6

Puttanesca sauce, a bold-flavored Italian sauce made of tomatoes, olives, capers, and anchovies, is an ideal partner for firm, meaty-textured swordfish. Keep your pantry stocked with the ingredients to make this dish anytime.

    4 (6-ounce) swordfish steaks (about 1½ inches thick)
    1 teaspoon olive oil
    ½ teaspoon freshly ground black pepper, divided
    Cooking spray
    2 tablespoons minced shallots
    1 teaspoon anchovy paste
    1 (14.5-ounce) can diced tomatoes with basil, garlic, and oregano, undrained
    ¼ cup chopped pitted kalamata olives
    1 teaspoon drained capers, chopped

1. Preheat broiler.
2. Brush fish with oil; sprinkle evenly with ¼ teaspoon pepper. Place fish on a broiler pan coated with cooking spray. Broil 10 minutes or until fish flakes easily when tested with a fork or until desired degree of doneness.
3. While fish broils, heat a medium saucepan over medium-high heat. Coat pan with cooking spray. Add shallots to pan. Cook 2 minutes or until tender, stirring frequently. Stir in anchovy paste; cook 30 seconds, stirring constantly. Stir in tomatoes, olives, capers, and remaining ¼ teaspoon pepper. Bring to a boil; cover, reduce heat, and simmer 8 minutes, stirring occasionally. Serve sauce over fish.
Yield: 4 servings (serving size: 1 steak and about ⅓ cup sauce).

Per serving: CALORIES 289 (33% from fat); FAT 10.5g (saturated fat 2.4g); PROTEIN 35.8g; CARBOHYDRATES 10.9g; FIBER 1g; CHOLESTEROL 71mg; IRON 3.1mg; SODIUM 928mg; CALCIUM 91mg

Sautéed Zucchini and Bell Peppers

prep: 3 minutes • **cook:** 8 minutes   *POINTS* value: 0

    1 teaspoon olive oil
    1 medium zucchini, quartered lengthwise and cut into 2-inch pieces
    1 cup refrigerated prechopped tricolor bell pepper
    1 garlic clove, minced
    ¼ teaspoon salt

1. Heat oil in a large nonstick skillet over medium-high heat. Add zucchini and remaining ingredients; sauté 7 minutes. **Yield:** 4 servings (serving size: ½ cup).

Per serving: CALORIES 28 (42% from fat); FAT 1g (saturated fat 0.2g); PROTEIN 1.1g; CARBOHYDRATES 3.9g; FIBER 0.8g; CHOLESTEROL 0mg; IRON 0.4mg; SODIUM 148mg; CALCIUM 14mg

Almond-Crusted Tilapia

prep: 5 minutes • **cook:** 7 minutes   ***POINTS*** value: 6

Reminiscent of a restaurant-style fish amandine, this recipe easily doubles to serve a small dinner party. Almonds add such a rich, nutty flavor to the tilapia that even the pickiest eater will think it is delicious. Serve with green beans and Mashed Red Potatoes with Chives.

- ¼   cup whole natural almonds
- 2   tablespoons dry breadcrumbs
- 1   teaspoon salt-free garlic and herb seasoning blend (such as Mrs. Dash)
- ⅛   teaspoon freshly ground black pepper
- 1½ teaspoons canola oil
- 1   tablespoon Dijon mustard
- 2   (6-ounce) tilapia fillets
  Chopped fresh parsley (optional)

1. Place first 4 ingredients in a blender or food processor; process 45 seconds or until finely ground. Transfer crumb mixture to a shallow dish.
2. Heat oil in a large nonstick skillet over medium heat. Brush mustard over both sides of fish; dredge in crumb mixture. Add tilapia fillets to pan; cook 3 minutes on each side or until fish flakes easily when tested with a fork or until desired degree of doneness. Sprinkle with parsley, if desired. **Yield:** 2 servings (serving size: 1 fillet).

Per serving: CALORIES 283 (36% from fat); FAT 11.2g (saturated fat 1.5g); PROTEIN 37.1g; CARBOHYDRATES 8.1g; FIBER 1.4g; CHOLESTEROL 85mg; IRON 1.3mg; SODIUM 321mg; CALCIUM 28mg

Menu
POINTS value
per serving: 8

Almond-Crusted Tilapia

Mashed Red Potatoes with Chives

1 cup green beans
POINTS value: 0

Game Plan

1. While potatoes cook:
- Prepare crumb mixture; dredge fish.
- Mince garlic and chop chives; chop parsley, if desired.
- Measure sour cream, milk, and yogurt-based spread.

2. While fish cooks:
- Mash potatoes to combine all ingredients.

Mashed Red Potatoes with Chives

prep: 1 minute • **cook:** 8 minutes   ***POINTS*** value: 2

- 1   red potato (about ½ pound)
- 1   garlic clove, minced
- 2   tablespoons reduced-fat sour cream
- 1½ tablespoons fat-free milk
- 1   tablespoon yogurt-based spread (such as Brummel & Brown)
- ⅛   teaspoon salt
- ⅛   teaspoon freshly ground black pepper
- 1½ teaspoons minced fresh chives

1. Scrub potato; place in a medium-sized microwave-safe bowl (do not pierce potato with a fork). Cover bowl with plastic wrap (do not allow plastic wrap to touch food); vent. Microwave at HIGH 8 minutes or until tender.
2. Add garlic and next 5 ingredients to potatoes. Mash to desired consistency. Stir in chives. **Yield:** 2 servings (serving size: about ½ cup).

Per serving: CALORIES 120 (27% from fat); FAT 4g (saturated fat 1.1g); PROTEIN 3g; CARBOHYDRATES 20g; FIBER 2g; CHOLESTEROL 4mg; IRON 1mg; SODIUM 208mg; CALCIUM 41mg

Menu
POINTS value
per serving: 8

**Seared Tuna with
Wasabi-Avocado Aïoli**

Spicy Cucumber Salad

Game Plan

1. Prepare cucumber salad.

2. Prepare aïoli.

3. Cook fish.

Seared Tuna with Wasabi-Avocado Aïoli

prep: 4 minutes • **cook:** 5 minutes   *POINTS* value: 7

Feel free to substitute salmon for the tuna. Be sure to prepare the avocado aïoli just before serving so that it doesn't discolor.

- ⅓ cup chopped peeled avocado (about ½ small)
- 2 tablespoons light mayonnaise
- 1 tablespoon fat-free sour cream
- 2 teaspoons fresh lemon juice
- ½ teaspoon wasabi (Japanese horseradish)
- ¼ teaspoon salt, divided
- 1 teaspoon canola oil
- 4 (6-ounce) tuna steaks (1 inch thick)
- ¼ teaspoon freshly ground black pepper

1. Combine first 5 ingredients and ⅛ teaspoon salt in a blender; process until smooth. Set aside.
2. Heat oil in a large nonstick skillet over medium-high heat. Sprinkle fish with ⅛ teaspoon salt and pepper. Cook fish 2 to 3 minutes on each side or until fish flakes easily when tested with a fork or until desired degree of doneness. Serve immediately with avocado aïoli. **Yield:** 4 servings (serving size: 1 steak and 2 tablespoons avocado aïoli).

Per serving: CALORIES 312 (42% from fat); FAT 14.5g (saturated fat 3.1g); PROTEIN 40.2g; CARBOHYDRATES 3g; FIBER 1.1g; CHOLESTEROL 67mg; IRON 1.8mg; SODIUM 293mg; CALCIUM 21mg

Spicy Cucumber Salad

prep: 10 minutes   *POINTS* value: 1

- ¼ cup rice vinegar
- 1 tablespoon sugar
- 1 teaspoon chili oil
- ½ teaspoon salt
- ¼ teaspoon crushed red pepper
- 3 medium cucumbers (about 1¼ pounds), peeled, seeded, and cut into ½-inch chunks
- ¼ cup minced shallots
- 1 tablespoon minced fresh cilantro

1. Combine first 5 ingredients in a medium bowl, stirring with a whisk. Add cucumber, shallots, and cilantro; toss well. **Yield:** 4 servings (serving size: about 1 cup).

Per serving: CALORIES 44 (25% from fat); FAT 1.2g (saturated fat 0.2g); PROTEIN 1.7g; CARBOHYDRATES 7.7g; FIBER 1.5g; CHOLESTEROL 0mg; IRON 0.7mg; SODIUM 293mg; CALCIUM 33mg

**English Muffins
Topped with Tomato-Chive
Baked Eggs** | page 11

Monte Cristo Sandwiches | page 19

**Waffles with
Berry Syrup** | page 20

Flounder with Warm Olive Salsa | page 26

Seared Salmon Fillets with
Edamame Succotash | page 29

Scallops and Pan-Roasted Tomatoes | page 54

Speedy Seafood Paella | page 58

Southwestern Rice and Veggie Cakes | page 67

Goat Cheese, Tomato,
and Basil Pizza | page 66

41

Sweet-and-Spicy Sirloin Steak | page 72

Taco Salad Pizza | page 80

Beef Tenderloin Steaks with
Red Wine–Mushroom Sauce | page 70

Parmesan-Crusted Pork Chops | page 86

Pork Medallions with
Sherry Glaze | page 83

Chicken-Veggie Noodle Bowl | page 92

**Grilled Chicken with Rustic
Mustard Cream** | page 102

Grilled Tuna over White Beans

prep: 5 minutes • **cook:** 4 minutes   *POINTS* value: 5

Cannellini beans, also known as white Italian kidney beans, marry with olive oil and lemon juice as typical ingredients in Tuscan cuisine.

- 1 (15.5-ounce) can cannellini beans, rinsed and drained
- ½ cup chopped red onion
- ¼ cup chopped fresh flat-leaf parsley
- 1½ tablespoons fresh lemon juice
- 2 teaspoons extra-virgin olive oil, divided
- ¾ teaspoon freshly ground black pepper, divided
- 4 (6-ounce) tuna steaks (1¼ inches thick)
- ½ teaspoon kosher salt
- Cooking spray
- 2 tablespoons chopped fresh parsley
- 4 lemon wedges

1. Prepare grill.

2. Combine beans, onion, ¼ cup parsley, lemon juice, 1 teaspoon oil, and ¼ teaspoon pepper in a medium bowl; toss well.

3. Brush fish with remaining 1 teaspoon olive oil; sprinkle evenly with salt and remaining ½ teaspoon pepper. Place fish on grill rack coated with cooking spray; grill 2 to 3 minutes on each side or until desired degree of doneness. Sprinkle fish evenly with parsley, and serve over beans with lemon wedges. **Yield:** 4 servings (serving size: 1 steak, ½ cup bean mixture, and 1 lemon wedge).

Per serving: CALORIES 266 (15% from fat); FAT 4.4g (saturated fat 0.9g); PROTEIN 40.7g; CARBOHYDRATES 13.5g; FIBER 3.6g; CHOLESTEROL 80mg; IRON 3.9mg; SODIUM 454mg; CALCIUM 87mg

---

Menu
POINTS value
per serving: 7

Grilled Tuna over White Beans

½ cup lemon sorbet
POINTS value: 2

Game Plan

1. While grill heats:
- Prepare white bean mixture.
- Cut lemon into wedges.
- Brush fish with oil; sprinkle with salt and pepper.

2. Cook fish.

3. Scoop sorbet into serving bowls.

Menu
POINTS value
per serving: 8

**Grilled Tuna Provençal
with Yogurt Sauce**

**Orzo with Spring Greens
and Rosemary**

Game Plan

1. While grill heats and water for pasta comes to a boil:
- Prepare yogurt sauce.
- Halve tomatoes and slice basil.
- Toast pine nuts.

2. While fish and tomatoes cook:
- Cook orzo.
- Chop mixed greens and mince rosemary.

3. Toss orzo.

Grilled Tuna Provençal with Yogurt Sauce

prep: 6 minutes • **cook:** 5 minutes   **POINTS** value: 5

If you can't find the assorted variety of cherry tomatoes, use the more familiar red ones.

- ½ cup Greek fat-free yogurt
- 2 garlic cloves, pressed
- ⅜ teaspoon salt, divided
- 4 teaspoons extra-virgin olive oil, divided
- 4 (6-ounce) Yellowfin tuna steaks (about 1 inch thick)

Olive oil–flavored cooking spray
- ½ teaspoon freshly ground black pepper
- 2 cups assorted-color cherry tomatoes, halved
- 3 tablespoons thinly sliced fresh basil

1. Prepare grill.
2. Combine yogurt, garlic, ⅛ teaspoon salt, and 2 teaspoons oil in a bowl; set aside.
3. Coat fish with cooking spray; sprinkle with remaining ¼ teaspoon salt and pepper. Combine tomatoes and remaining 2 teaspoons olive oil in an 8-inch square pan.
4. Place fish and pan on grill rack coated with cooking spray. Grill fish 2 to 3 minutes on each side or until desired degree of doneness. Grill tomatoes 5 minutes or until soft.
5. Toss basil into tomato mixture. Place fish on 4 plates. Top with tomato mixture; serve with yogurt sauce. **Yield:** 4 servings (serving size: 1 steak, ½ cup tomatoes, and 2 tablespoons yogurt sauce).

Per serving: CALORIES 256 (23% from fat); FAT 6.5g (saturated fat 1.1g); PROTEIN 43.1g; CARBOHYDRATES 4.8g; FIBER 1.1g; CHOLESTEROL 77mg; IRON 1.6mg; SODIUM 295mg; CALCIUM 61mg

Orzo with Spring Greens and Rosemary

prep: 1 minute • **cook:** 10 minutes   **POINTS** value: 3

- ¾ cup uncooked orzo (rice-shaped pasta)
- 1 cup spring greens mix, coarsely chopped
- 1 tablespoon pine nuts, toasted
- 1 tablespoon extra-virgin olive oil
- ½ teaspoon minced fresh rosemary
- ¼ teaspoon salt

1. Cook orzo according to package directions, omitting salt and fat. Drain pasta; place in a medium bowl.
2. Add greens mix and remaining ingredients, tossing well. **Yield:** 4 servings (serving size: about ⅔ cup).

Per serving: CALORIES 166 (30% from fat); FAT 5.6g (saturated fat 0.6g); PROTEIN 4.5g; CARBOHYDRATES 24.6g; FIBER 1.5g; CHOLESTEROL 0mg; IRON 0.4mg; SODIUM 149mg; CALCIUM 9mg

Trout Grenobloise

prep: 2 minutes • **cook:** 13 minutes   ***POINTS*** value: 7

Literally translated "of Grenoble," a city in southeastern France, Grenobloise is a classic French sauce consisting of lemon juice, capers, and browned butter. Here, we use our version of this sauce in a simple trout dish, but it can be paired with different types of fish, if desired.

    2   teaspoons olive oil, divided
    4   (6-ounce) trout fillets
    ¼   teaspoon freshly ground black pepper
    ⅛   teaspoon salt
    Cooking spray
    1   tablespoon butter
    1   tablespoon fresh lemon juice
    2   teaspoons capers

1. Heat 1 teaspoon oil in a large nonstick skillet over medium-high heat until hot. Sprinkle fish with pepper and salt. Add half of fish to pan, skin side down, and cook 4 minutes or until skin is crispy. Coat flesh side with cooking spray; turn fish, and cook 1 minute or until fish flakes easily when tested with a fork. Remove from pan, and keep warm. Repeat with remaining 1 teaspoon oil and remaining half of fish.
2. Melt butter in pan over medium heat; cook 1 minute or until golden brown. Add lemon juice and capers. Spoon sauce over fish, and serve immediately. **Yield:** 4 servings (serving size: 1 fillet and 1½ teaspoons sauce).

Per serving: CALORIES 281 (45% from fat); FAT 14.2g (saturated fat 4.7g); PROTEIN 35.6g; CARBOHYDRATES 0.5g; FIBER 0.1g; CHOLESTEROL 108mg; IRON 0.5mg; SODIUM 200mg; CALCIUM 115mg

Balsamic-Glazed Green Beans

prep: 2 minutes • **cook:** 10 minutes   ***POINTS*** value: 1

    1   (12-ounce) package trimmed green beans
    1   tablespoon butter
    3   tablespoons minced shallots (about 2)
    2   garlic cloves, minced
    ¼   cup balsamic vinegar
    ½   teaspoon salt
    ¼   teaspoon freshly ground black pepper

1. Microwave green beans according to package directions.
2. Melt butter in a large skillet over medium heat. Add shallots and garlic; cook, stirring constantly, 2 minutes. Stir in vinegar, salt, and pepper; cook 1 minute. Add beans, tossing to coat. **Yield:** 4 servings (serving size: ¾ cup).

Per serving: CALORIES 76 (37% from fat); FAT 3.1g (saturated fat 1.9g); PROTEIN 2g; CARBOHYDRATES 11.1g; FIBER 2.8g; CHOLESTEROL 8mg; IRON 0.8mg; SODIUM 515mg; CALCIUM 48mg

---

Menu
POINTS value
per serving: 8

Trout Grenobloise

Balsamic-Glazed Green Beans

Game Plan

1. Mince garlic and shallots; juice fresh lemon.

2. While fish cooks:
  • Microwave green beans.

3. Toss green beans with balsamic vinegar glaze.

Menu
POINTS value
per serving: 5

Linguine with Clam Sauce

1 cup mixed greens salad with
fat-free balsamic vinaigrette
POINTS value: 0

Game Plan

1. While water for pasta comes to
a boil:
- Mince shallots and garlic;
juice lemon.

2. While pasta cooks:
- Sauté shallots and garlic.
- Chop parsley.

3. While clam mixture comes to a
boil:
- Assemble salad.

4. Toss pasta.

Linguine with Clam Sauce

prep: 7 minutes • **cook:** 10 minutes   *POINTS* value: 5

Make great use of canned clams in this tasty combination of pasta, clams, and white wine sauce.

½   (9-ounce) package refrigerated linguine
2   (6.5-ounce) cans chopped clams, undrained
1½ tablespoons olive oil
⅓   cup minced shallots (about 2 medium)
1   tablespoon minced fresh garlic
½   cup dry white wine
2   teaspoons fresh lemon juice
½   teaspoon black pepper
¼   teaspoon salt
¼   teaspoon crushed red pepper
⅓   cup chopped fresh parsley

1. Cook pasta according to package directions, omitting salt and fat; drain well.
2. While pasta cooks, drain clams, reserving ½ cup clam juice. Heat oil in a large nonstick skillet over medium-high heat. Add shallots and garlic; sauté 3 minutes or until shallots are tender. Add reserved ½ cup clam juice, wine, and next 4 ingredients; bring to a boil. Stir in clams and parsley. Reduce heat, and simmer 1 minute.
3. Combine pasta and clam mixture; toss well, and serve immediately. **Yield:** 3 servings (serving size: 1 cup).

Per serving: CALORIES 251 (28% from fat); FAT 7.9g (saturated fat 1.1g); PROTEIN 11.9g; CARBOHYDRATES 30.3g; FIBER 2.2g; CHOLESTEROL 47mg; IRON 3.3mg; SODIUM 772mg; CALCIUM 31mg

Scallops in Buttery Wine Sauce

prep: 1 minute • **cook:** 8 minutes   ***POINTS*** value: 5

Pat the scallops dry with a paper towel to remove any excess moisture before searing. This step ensures a nicely browned exterior.

    1½   pounds large sea scallops
     1   tablespoon olive oil
     ½   cup dry white wine
    1½   teaspoons chopped fresh tarragon
     ¼   teaspoon salt
     1   tablespoon butter
Freshly ground black pepper (optional)

1. Pat scallops dry with paper towels. Heat oil in a large nonstick skillet over medium-high heat; add scallops. Cook 3 minutes on each side or until done. Transfer scallops to a serving platter; keep warm.
2. Add white wine, tarragon, and salt to pan, scraping pan to loosen browned bits. Boil 1 minute. Remove from heat; add butter, stirring until butter melts. Pour sauce over scallops. Sprinkle with pepper, if desired; serve immediately. **Yield:** 4 servings (serving size: about 3 scallops and about 1 tablespoon sauce).

Per serving: CALORIES 225 (30% from fat); FAT 8g (saturated fat 2.4g); PROTEIN 28.6g; CARBOHYDRATES 4.7g; FIBER 0g; CHOLESTEROL 64mg; IRON 0.6mg; SODIUM 441mg; CALCIUM 45mg

Asparagus with Feta and Oregano

prep: 2 minutes • **cook:** 6 minutes   ***POINTS*** value: 1

     1   cup water
     1   pound asparagus spears, trimmed
     1   teaspoon extra-virgin olive oil
    1½   teaspoons chopped fresh oregano
     ¼   teaspoon salt
     3   tablespoons crumbled feta cheese

1. Bring 1 cup water to a boil in a large nonstick skillet; add asparagus. Cover, reduce heat, and simmer 4 to 5 minutes or until asparagus is crisp-tender. Drain well; place on a serving platter.
2. Drizzle oil over asparagus. Sprinkle with oregano and salt; toss well. Sprinkle with cheese. **Yield:** 4 servings (serving size: ¼ of asparagus spears).

Per serving: CALORIES 40 (45% from fat); FAT 2g (saturated fat 0.7g); PROTEIN 2.7g; CARBOHYDRATES 3.1g; FIBER 1.6g; CHOLESTEROL 2mg; IRON 1.5mg; SODIUM 222mg; CALCIUM 35mg

---

Menu
POINTS value
per serving: 6

Scallops in Buttery Wine Sauce

Asparagus with Feta and Oregano

Game Plan

1. While water for asparagus comes to a boil:
  • Trim asparagus.
  • Chop oregano and tarragon.

2. While scallops cook:
  • Cook asparagus.

3. Prepare wine sauce.

4. Combine asparagus with oil, seasonings, and cheese.

pictured on page 38

Scallops and Pan-Roasted Tomatoes

prep: 4 minutes • **cook:** 16 minutes   *POINTS* value: 5

This simple dish features juicy scallops and grape tomatoes that, after pan-roasting, literally burst with fresh flavor.

- ¾ pound sea scallops (about 6 large scallops)
- ⅛ teaspoon salt
- ⅛ teaspoon freshly ground black pepper
- Olive oil–flavored cooking spray
- 1 pint grape tomatoes
- ¼ cup chopped pitted kalamata olives
- 2 teaspoons chopped fresh oregano
- 1 teaspoon fresh lemon juice
- Fresh thyme sprigs (optional)

1. Pat scallops dry with paper towels to remove excess moisture. Sprinkle scallops with salt and pepper.

2. Heat a large nonstick skillet over medium-high heat. Coat pan with cooking spray. Add scallops and tomatoes. Cook scallops 3 minutes on each side or until done. Remove scallops; keep warm.

3. Cover pan, and continue cooking tomatoes 10 minutes or until they brown and begin to burst. Remove from heat; stir in olives and oregano. Serve scallops over tomato mixture. Drizzle lemon juice over scallops. Garnish with thyme sprigs, if desired. **Yield:** 2 servings (serving size: 3 scallops and about ½ cup tomatoes).

Per serving: CALORIES 232 (26% from fat); FAT 6.7g (saturated fat 0.7g); PROTEIN 30.2g; CARBOHYDRATES 12g; FIBER 2g; CHOLESTEROL 56mg; IRON 1mg; SODIUM 718mg; CALCIUM 69mg

---

Menu
POINTS value
per serving: 7

Scallops and Pan-Roasted Tomatoes

½ cup cooked orzo
POINTS value: 2

Game Plan

1. While water for orzo comes to a boil:
- Sear scallops.

2. While orzo cooks:
- Cook tomatoes.
- Chop olives and oregano; juice lemon.

Shrimp with Avocado Salsa

prep: 10 minutes • **cook:** 4 minutes   ***POINTS*** value: 5

Cilantro delivers a fresh, pungent contrast to the milder avocado and shrimp.

1	diced peeled avocado
2	tablespoons minced fresh cilantro
2	tablespoons minced green onions
1	tablespoon fresh lime juice
⅛	teaspoon salt
1½	pounds peeled and deveined large shrimp
1	tablespoon olive oil
¼	teaspoon salt
¼	teaspoon freshly ground black pepper
¼	teaspoon ground cumin

1. Combine first 5 ingredients in a small bowl; stir gently.
2. Toss shrimp and next 4 ingredients in a medium bowl.
3. Heat a large nonstick skillet over medium-high heat. Add shrimp mixture; sauté 3 minutes or until done. Serve with salsa. **Yield:** 4 servings (serving size: about 1 cup shrimp and about 2 tablespoons salsa).

Per serving: CALORIES 242 (47% from fat); FAT 12.6g (saturated fat 2.1g); PROTEIN 28.2g; CARBOHYDRATES 4.4g; FIBER 2.7g; CHOLESTEROL 252mg; IRON 4.6mg; SODIUM 514mg; CALCIUM 61mg

Chili-Lime Corn on the Cob

prep: 3 minutes • **cook:** 8 minutes   ***POINTS*** value: 3

4	ears shucked corn
2	tablespoons butter
½	teaspoon chili powder
½	teaspoon grated lime rind
¼	teaspoon salt
¼	teaspoon freshly ground black pepper

1. Place corn in a microwave-safe dish; cover dish with wax paper. Microwave at HIGH 7 minutes or until tender.
2. Place butter in a small microwave-safe bowl. Microwave at HIGH 15 seconds or until butter melts. Stir in chili powder, lime rind, salt, and pepper. Brush butter mixture evenly over cooked corn. **Yield:** 4 servings (serving size: 1 ear).

Per serving: CALORIES 131 (47% from fat); FAT 7g (saturated fat 3.8g); PROTEIN 3g; CARBOHYDRATES 18.1g; FIBER 2.7g; CHOLESTEROL 15mg; IRON 0.5mg; SODIUM 209mg; CALCIUM 7mg

Menu
POINTS value
per serving: 8

Shrimp with Avocado Salsa

Chili-Lime Corn on the Cob

Game Plan

1. While corn cooks:
 • Prepare avocado salsa.

2. While shrimp cooks:
 • Prepare chili-lime butter.

Menu
POINTS value
per serving: 6

Grilled Spicy Asian Shrimp

Minted Sugar Snap Peas

½ cup precooked Jasmine rice
POINTS value: 2

Game Plan

1. While grill heats:
   • Cook rice in microwave.
   • Prepare sauce for shrimp.
   • Thread shrimp onto skewers; brush with sauce.

2. Cook shrimp.

3. Prepare sugar snap peas.

Grilled Spicy Asian Shrimp

prep: 7 minutes • **cook:** 6 minutes   *POINTS* value: 3

Precubed pineapple would make a sweet ending to this spicy meal. One cup has a *POINTS* value of 1.

- ¼ cup chopped fresh cilantro, divided
- 2 tablespoons chili garlic sauce (such as Lee Kum Kee)
- 1 tablespoon rice vinegar
- 1 teaspoon grated peeled fresh ginger
- 1 teaspoon fish sauce
- 1 teaspoon dark sesame oil
- 1½ pounds peeled and deveined shrimp (about 46)
  Cooking spray
- 4 lime wedges

1. Prepare grill.

2. Combine 2 tablespoons cilantro and next 5 ingredients in a small bowl, stirring with a whisk.

3. Thread shrimp evenly onto 4 (12-inch) metal skewers. Brush both sides of shrimp with sauce. Place skewers on grill rack coated with cooking spray. Grill 3 minutes on each side or until shrimp are done, brushing frequently with remaining spicy sauce. Sprinkle shrimp evenly with remaining 2 tablespoons cilantro, and serve with lime wedges. **Yield:** 4 servings (serving size: 1 skewer and 1 lime wedge).

Per serving: CALORIES 138 (17% from fat); FAT 2.6g (saturated fat 0.5g); PROTEIN 27.2g; CARBOHYDRATES 0.9g; FIBER 0g; CHOLESTEROL 252mg; IRON 4mg; SODIUM 490mg; CALCIUM 51mg

Minted Sugar Snap Peas

prep: 2 minutes • **cook:** 3 minutes   *POINTS* value: 1

- 1 teaspoon canola oil
- 1 (8-ounce) package fresh sugar snap peas
- 1 tablespoon chopped fresh mint
- 1 teaspoon grated orange rind
- ¼ teaspoon salt

1. Heat oil in a large nonstick skillet over medium-high heat; add peas. Sauté 2 minutes or just until peas are crisp-tender. Stir in mint, orange rind, and salt. **Yield:** 4 servings (serving size: ½ cup).

Per serving: CALORIES 38 (28% from fat); FAT 1g (saturated fat 0.1g); PROTEIN 1.4g; CARBOHYDRATES 4.9g; FIBER 1.4g; CHOLESTEROL 0mg; IRON 0.8mg; SODIUM 152mg; CALCIUM 42mg

Curried Shrimp over Garlic-Basil Coconut Rice

prep: 2 minutes • **cook:** 15 minutes • **other:** 5 minutes   *POINTS* value: 8

The bright, tart flavor of freshly squeezed lime juice balances the spicy and sweet sauce that coats the shrimp. Serve with steamed broccoli for a side with a *POINTS* value of 0 per serving.

- 1   (6.7-ounce) package Jasmine rice mix with garlic, basil, and coconut (such as Taste of Thai)
- ½   teaspoon curry powder
- 1½ pounds peeled and deveined large shrimp
- 1   teaspoon olive oil
- Cooking spray
- 2   garlic cloves, minced
- ½   cup low-sugar orange marmalade
- 2   tablespoons water
- 2   tablespoons chopped fresh cilantro
- 4   lime wedges

1. Cook rice according to package directions, omitting salt and fat.

2. While rice cooks, sprinkle curry powder evenly over shrimp, tossing to coat. Heat oil in a large nonstick skillet over medium-high heat. Coat shrimp with cooking spray, and add to pan; sauté 3 minutes. Add garlic; sauté 2 minutes or until shrimp are done.

3. Add orange marmalade and 2 tablespoons water to shrimp mixture. Cook over medium heat until marmalade melts, tossing to coat shrimp.

4. Divide rice evenly among 4 bowls. Spoon shrimp mixture evenly over rice, and sprinkle with cilantro. Serve with lime wedges. **Yield:** 4 servings (serving size: about ¾ cup shrimp mixture, about ½ cup rice, and 1 lime wedge).

Per serving: CALORIES 379 (14% from fat); FAT 5.7g (saturated fat 2.7g); PROTEIN 30g; CARBOHYDRATES 49g; FIBER 1.1g; CHOLESTEROL 252mg; IRON 4mg; SODIUM 667mg; CALCIUM 74mg

---

Menu
POINTS value
per serving: 8

Curried Shrimp over Garlic-Basil Coconut Rice

1 cup steamed broccoli
POINTS value: 0

Game Plan

1. While rice cooks:
- Mince garlic.
- Chop cilantro.
- Cut lime into wedges.

2. While shrimp cook:
- Steam broccoli.

pictured on page 39

Speedy Seafood Paella

prep: 5 minutes • **cook:** 15 minutes   ***POINTS*** value: 6

Game Plan

1. Slice sausage.

2. While sausage mixture cooks:
• Cook rice.
• Mince garlic; measure bell pepper and onion.

3. While sausage and bell pepper mix cooks:
• Measure remaining paella ingredients.

4. Simmer paella.

Paella is a traditional Spanish specialty that combines saffron-flavored rice with meat, shellfish, onion, peas, and tomatoes. We've substituted turmeric for pricier saffron and cut down on prep time without sacrificing flavor.

  2 (10-ounce) packages frozen cooked brown rice (such as Birds Eye)
  2 teaspoons olive oil
  7 ounces smoked turkey sausage (such as Butterball), halved lengthwise and cut into ½-inch-thick slices
  3 cups prechopped bell pepper mix
2½ cups prechopped onion
  3 garlic cloves, minced
  ½ teaspoon ground turmeric
  ¼ teaspoon ground red pepper
  1 (14.5-ounce) can diced tomatoes with basil, garlic, and oregano, undrained
  ¾ pound peeled and deveined medium shrimp
  2 cups chopped cooked chicken breast
  ¼ teaspoon freshly ground black pepper
  ¾ cup frozen petite green peas, thawed

1. Cook rice according to package directions.
2. While rice cooks, heat oil in a large deep skillet over medium-high heat. Add sausage; cook 3 minutes or until browned, stirring occasionally. Add bell pepper mix, onion, and garlic; cook 4 minutes or until vegetables are tender. Stir in turmeric and red pepper; cook 1 minute, stirring constantly. Add cooked rice, tomatoes, and remaining ingredients. Bring to a boil; cover, reduce heat, and simmer 4 minutes or until shrimp are done. Serve immediately. **Yield:** 8 servings (serving size: about 1½ cups).

Per serving: CALORIES 305 (19% from fat); FAT 6.6g (saturated fat 1.8g); PROTEIN 27.2g; CARBOHYDRATES 32.2g; FIBER 4.2g; CHOLESTEROL 102mg; IRON 3.3mg; SODIUM 570mg; CALCIUM 102mg

Meatless Main Dishes

Menu
POINTS value
per serving: 8

**Refried Bean Poblanos
with Cheese**

Creamy Chipotle Wedge Salad

Game Plan

1. While chiles cook:
   • Prepare bean mixture.

2. While stuffed chiles cook:
   • Prepare dressing for salad.

3. Assemble salad.

Refried Bean Poblanos with Cheese

prep: 2 minutes • **cook:** 6 minutes

POINTS value: 6

Poblano chiles grown in a hot, dry climate can be more intense than others, so the spiciness of this dish depends on the heat of your peppers.

   4   medium poblano chiles, halved and seeded
   1   (16-ounce) can fat-free refried beans
   1   (8.8-ounce) package precooked long-grain rice (such as Uncle Ben's Original Ready Rice)
   ½   cup picante sauce
   1   cup (4 ounces) preshredded reduced-fat 4-cheese Mexican blend cheese
   Chopped fresh cilantro (optional)

1. Place chile halves, cut sides up, on a round microwave-safe plate. Cover with wax paper; microwave at HIGH 3 minutes.
2. While chiles cook, combine beans, rice, and picante sauce in a medium bowl, stirring well. Spoon bean mixture evenly into chile halves. Cover with wax paper; microwave at HIGH 2 minutes. Uncover chiles, sprinkle each half with 2 tablespoons cheese, and microwave at HIGH 1 to 2 minutes or until cheese melts. Sprinkle evenly with cilantro, if desired. **Yield:** 4 servings (serving size: 2 stuffed chile halves).

Per serving: CALORIES 303 (19% from fat); FAT 6g (saturated fat 3.1g); PROTEIN 17g; CARBOHYDRATES 45.4g; FIBER 7.7g; CHOLESTEROL 10mg; IRON 0.7mg; SODIUM 960mg; CALCIUM 232mg

Creamy Chipotle Wedge Salad

prep: 5 minutes

POINTS value: 2

   ½   cup refrigerated light ranch dressing (such as Naturally Fresh)
   1   chipotle chile, canned in adobo sauce
   1   green onion, cut into 2-inch pieces
   ½   head iceberg lettuce, cored and quartered

1. Place first 3 ingredients in a blender; process until smooth. Serve chipotle dressing over lettuce wedges. **Yield:** 4 servings (serving size: 1 lettuce wedge and 2½ tablespoons dressing).

Per serving: CALORIES 90 (70% from fat); FAT 7g (saturated fat 0.6g); PROTEIN 1g; CARBOHYDRATES 5.8g; FIBER 1.2g; CHOLESTEROL 8mg; IRON 0.5mg; SODIUM 338mg; CALCIUM 23mg

Vegetarian Enchiladas

prep: 5 minutes • **cook:** 15 minutes

POINTS value: 4

You'll love the extra kick the spicy refried beans give to these meatless enchiladas.

  ¾ cup fat-free spicy refried beans
  4 (8-inch) flour tortillas
  1 cup frozen meatless burger crumbles (such as Morningstar Farms)
  ¾ cup enchilada sauce
  ½ cup (2 ounces) reduced-fat shredded sharp Cheddar cheese
  Chopped green onions (optional)

1. Preheat oven to 400°.
2. Spread 3 tablespoons beans over each tortilla, leaving a ¾-inch border around edges. Sprinkle ¼ cup burger crumbles down center of each tortilla; roll up tortillas. Arrange tortillas, seam sides down, in an 8-inch square baking dish. Pour enchilada sauce over tortillas; sprinkle with cheese.
3. Bake at 400° for 15 minutes or until bubbly and cheese melts. Top with green onions, if desired. **Yield:** 4 servings (serving size: 1 enchilada).

Per serving: CALORIES 242 (18% from fat); FAT 4.8g (saturated fat 1.6g); PROTEIN 13.8g; CARBOHYDRATES 35.2g; FIBER 5g; CHOLESTEROL 8mg; IRON 1.4mg; SODIUM 982mg; CALCIUM 151mg

Menu
POINTS value
per serving: 8

Vegetarian Enchilada

**Golden Onion and
Corn Rice Pilaf**

Game Plan

1. While oven preheats:
• Assemble enchiladas.

2. While enchiladas cook:
• Prepare pilaf.

Golden Onion and Corn Rice Pilaf

prep: 1 minute • **cook:** 8 minutes

POINTS value: 4

  1 (8.8-ounce) package precooked whole-grain brown rice (such as Uncle Ben's Ready Rice)
  Cooking spray
  1 cup frozen whole-kernel corn
  ½ cup prechopped onion
  1 tablespoon butter
  ½ teaspoon ground cumin
  ¼ teaspoon salt
  ¼ teaspoon black pepper

1. Microwave rice according to package directions.
2. While rice cooks, heat a large nonstick skillet over medium-high heat. Coat pan with cooking spray. Add corn and onion; cook 4 minutes or until browned, stirring constantly.
3. Add butter and cumin; cook 2 minutes, stirring constantly. Remove from heat. Add cooked rice, salt, and pepper; toss well. **Yield:** 4 servings (serving size: about ½ cup).

Per serving: CALORIES 191 (23% from fat); FAT 4.8g (saturated fat 1.9g); PROTEIN 4.1g; CARBOHYDRATES 30.1g; FIBER 2.5g; CHOLESTEROL 8mg; IRON 0.9mg; SODIUM 178mg; CALCIUM 10mg

Menu
POINTS value
per serving: 6

Broccoli and Ginger Tofu Stir-Fry

1 cup prechopped tropical fruit
POINTS value: 1

Game Plan

1. While water for pasta comes to a boil:
- Cut tofu into cubes; mince ginger and garlic.

2. While pasta, vegetables, and tofu cook:
- Prepare broth mixture.

3. While broth mixture cooks with tofu mixture:
- Drain pasta.

4. Combine vegetables with broth and tofu mixture.

Broccoli and Ginger Tofu Stir-Fry

prep: 6 minutes • **cook:** 13 minutes   **POINTS** value: 5

Look for containers of prechopped mixed tropical fruit, such as pineapple and kiwi, in the produce section of your supermarket.

6 ounces uncooked angel hair pasta
1 (12-ounce) bag fresh-cut vegetable stir-fry blend (such as Eat Smart)
Cooking spray
1 (20-ounce) package superfirm tofu, drained and cut into ½-inch cubes
¾ cup organic vegetable broth
¼ cup less-sodium soy sauce (such as Kikkoman)
3 tablespoons dry white wine
1 tablespoon cornstarch
2 teaspoons minced peeled fresh ginger
3 garlic cloves, minced

1. Cook pasta according to package directions, omitting salt and fat; drain and keep warm.
2. While pasta cooks, microwave vegetables according to package directions and heat a large nonstick skillet over medium-high heat. Coat pan with cooking spray. Add tofu, and sauté 7 minutes or until browned.
3. Combine broth and next 5 ingredients, stirring with a whisk. Add broth mixture to pan, and cook 2 minutes or until slightly thick. Remove pan from heat, and stir in vegetables. Serve over hot pasta. **Yield:** 4 servings (serving size: 1½ cups tofu mixture and ¾ cup pasta).

Per serving: CALORIES 267 (13% from fat); FAT 4g (saturated fat 0.4g); PROTEIN 14.1g; CARBOHYDRATES 41.7g; FIBER 3g; CHOLESTEROL 0mg; IRON 2.6mg; SODIUM 729mg; CALCIUM 166mg

Vietnamese Noodle-Vegetable Toss

prep: 7 minutes • **cook**: 5 minutes • **other**: 3 minutes   ***POINTS*** value: 8

Vietnamese cuisine is truly light Asian food. Rice noodles make this a hearty dish without leaving you feeling overly full. Covering the pot for the water will ensure that it comes to a boil quickly.

6 cups water
6 ounces uncooked linguine-style rice noodles (such as Thai Kitchen)
1 tablespoon sugar
2 tablespoons water
1 tablespoon fish sauce
1 tablespoon fresh lime juice
2 cups packaged tricolor slaw mix
1 cup grated English cucumber
1 cup fresh bean sprouts
1 cup fresh cilantro leaves
½ cup chopped unsalted, dry-roasted peanuts

1. Bring 6 cups water to a boil in a large saucepan. Remove from heat; add rice noodles. Let soak 3 minutes or until tender. Drain.
2. While noodles soak, combine sugar and next 3 ingredients in a small bowl, stirring well with a whisk.
3. Combine noodles, slaw mix, and next 3 ingredients in a large bowl. Toss with sugar mixture. Sprinkle with peanuts. Serve immediately. **Yield:** 3 servings (serving size: 1⅓ cups).

Per serving: CALORIES 388 (28% from fat); FAT 12g (saturated fat 1.7g); PROTEIN 10.7g; CARBOHYDRATES 61g; FIBER 3.8g; CHOLESTEROL 0mg; IRON 2mg; SODIUM 397mg; CALCIUM 49mg

---

Menu
POINTS value
per serving: 8

**Vietnamese
Noodle-Vegetable Toss**

Game Plan

1. While water for noodles comes to a boil:
  • Grate English cucumber; chop peanuts.

2. While noodles soak:
  • Prepare sugar mixture.
  • Measure slaw mix, bean sprouts, and cilantro leaves.

3. Toss noodle mixture; sprinkle with peanuts.

Menu
POINTS value
per serving: 7

Creamy Macaroni and Cheese

Green Beans with
Country Mustard and Herbs

Game Plan

1. While water for pasta comes to a boil:
- Chop parsley and oregano for beans.

2. While pasta cooks:
- Coat ramekins.
- Preheat broiler.
- Prepare milk mixture.
- Prepare and measure cheeses.
- Cook beans.

3. While Creamy Macaroni and Cheese cooks:
- Prepare butter mixture for beans.

4. Toss beans.

Creamy Macaroni and Cheese

prep: 2 minutes • **cook:** 16 minutes   *POINTS* value: 6

We used multigrain pasta to add fiber to this creamy comfort food and low-fat dairy products to reduce the calories and fat.

  2 cups uncooked multigrain macaroni (such as Barilla PLUS)
Cooking spray
1½ cups fat-free milk
  3 tablespoons all-purpose flour
  3 ounces light processed cheese (such as Velveeta Light), cubed
  1 cup (4 ounces) reduced-fat shredded extra-sharp Cheddar cheese (such as Cracker Barrel), divided
¼ teaspoon salt
¼ teaspoon black pepper

1. Cook macaroni in boiling water 8 minutes, omitting salt and fat. Drain and set aside.
2. Coat 5 (8-ounce) broiler-safe ramekins or baking dishes with cooking spray.
3. Preheat broiler.
4. While pasta cooks, combine milk and flour in a large saucepan, stirring with a whisk until blended. Cook over medium-high heat 10 minutes or until thick, stirring constantly. Remove pan from heat; add processed cheese, ¾ cup Cheddar cheese, salt, and pepper, stirring until cheeses melt. Stir in macaroni.
5. Spoon macaroni mixture into prepared ramekins; sprinkle with remaining ¼ cup Cheddar cheese. Set ramekins on a baking sheet; broil 3 minutes or until cheese melts. **Yield:** 5 servings (serving size: 1 ramekin).

Per serving: CALORIES 323 (23% from fat); FAT 8.4g (saturated fat 4.1g); PROTEIN 19.8g; CARBOHYDRATES 40.7g; FIBER 3.4g; CHOLESTEROL 19mg; IRON 2.4mg; SODIUM 633mg; CALCIUM 368mg

Green Beans with Country Mustard and Herbs

prep: 2 minutes • **cook:** 5 minutes   *POINTS* value: 1

  1 (12-ounce) package trimmed green beans
  1 tablespoon butter
  2 tablespoons chopped fresh parsley
1½ teaspoons chopped fresh oregano
  2 teaspoons whole-grain Dijon mustard
¼ teaspoon salt

1. Microwave green beans according to package directions.
2. While beans cook, place butter and next 4 ingredients in a serving bowl. Add beans; toss gently until butter melts. **Yield:** 4 servings (serving size: ½ cup).

Per serving: CALORIES 55 (49% from fat); FAT 3g (saturated fat 1.8g); PROTEIN 1.7g; CARBOHYDRATES 6.8g; FIBER 3g; CHOLESTEROL 8mg; IRON 1mg; SODIUM 232mg; CALCIUM 37mg

Ravioli with Sun-Dried Tomato Cream Sauce

prep: 4 minutes • **cook:** 8 minutes

POINTS value: 6

Menu
POINTS value
per serving: 7

Ravioli with Sun-Dried Tomato
Cream Sauce

Sautéed Zucchini Spears

Game Plan

1. Quarter mushrooms, chop onion, and cut zucchini.

2. While ravioli cooks:
   • Sauté mushrooms and onion; cook sauce.
   • Prepare zucchini.

3. Assemble ravioli.

1 (18-ounce) package frozen steam-and-eat small cheese ravioli (such as Rosetto)
2 teaspoons olive oil
1 (8-ounce) package baby portobello mushrooms, quartered
½ cup coarsely chopped onion
½ teaspoon all-purpose flour
½ cup plus 2 tablespoons half-and-half
2 tablespoons sun-dried tomato pesto (such as Classico)
¼ teaspoon salt
¼ teaspoon black pepper
¼ cup (1 ounce) shaved fresh Asiago cheese
Basil leaves (optional)

1. Microwave ravioli according to package directions.
2. While ravioli cooks, heat oil in a large nonstick skillet over medium-high heat. Add mushrooms and onion; sauté 3 to 4 minutes or until richly browned. Combine flour and next 4 ingredients in a small bowl, stirring until smooth. Add to pan, stirring well. Cook over medium-low heat 2 minutes or until mixture thickens slightly.
3. Divide cooked ravioli evenly among 4 shallow bowls or plates; spoon mushroom mixture evenly over ravioli. Sprinkle evenly with cheese; garnish with basil, if desired. **Yield:** 4 servings (serving size: 13 ravioli, about ½ cup mushroom sauce, and 1 tablespoon cheese).

Per serving: CALORIES 306 (26% from fat); FAT 9g (saturated fat 3.8g); PROTEIN 13.8g; CARBOHYDRATES 41.5g; FIBER 3.1g; CHOLESTEROL 21mg; IRON 2.9mg; SODIUM 583mg; CALCIUM 199mg

Sautéed Zucchini Spears

prep: 3 minutes • **cook:** 6 minutes

POINTS value: 1

3 medium zucchini (about 1 pound)
1½ teaspoons olive oil
½ cup coarsely chopped onion
¼ teaspoon salt
⅛ teaspoon black pepper

1. Cut zucchini in half lengthwise; cut each half crosswise into 2 pieces. Cut each zucchini piece into 3 spears.
2. Heat oil in a large nonstick skillet over medium-high heat; add zucchini and onion. Sauté 5 to 6 minutes or until vegetables are lightly browned. Sprinkle with salt and pepper; toss well. **Yield:** 4 servings (serving size: about ¾ cup).

Per serving: CALORIES 47 (38% from fat); FAT 2g (saturated fat 0.3g); PROTEIN 2g; CARBOHYDRATES 6.8g; FIBER 2g; CHOLESTEROL 0mg; IRON 0.6mg; SODIUM 161mg; CALCIUM 27mg

pictured on page 41

Goat Cheese, Tomato, and Basil Pizza

prep: 5 minutes • **cook:** 10 minutes

POINTS value: 5

This pizza gets its robust taste from creamy goat cheese and juicy, sweet grape tomatoes. Vary the flavor by substituting your favorite pasta sauce.

1 (10-ounce) Italian cheese-flavored thin pizza crust (such as Boboli)
Cooking spray
1 cup marinara sauce (such as Barilla)
4 ounces (about 1 cup) crumbled goat cheese
¾ cup grape tomatoes, halved lengthwise
2 tablespoons fresh basil leaves

1. Preheat oven to 450°.
2. Place pizza crust on an ungreased baking sheet; lightly coat crust with cooking spray. Pour ½ cup sauce onto several thicknesses of paper towels. Carefully scrape sauce over dry portions of paper towels until thick, using a rubber spatula. Spread thickened sauce evenly over crust. Repeat procedure with remaining ½ cup sauce.
3. Sprinkle cheese and tomatoes over crust. Slide pizza off pan directly onto oven rack.
4. Bake at 450° for 10 minutes or until crust is golden and crisp. Carefully slide pizza from oven rack back onto pan using a spatula. Sprinkle pizza with basil; cut into 6 slices. **Yield:** 6 servings (serving size: 1 slice).

Per serving: CALORIES 250 (35% from fat); FAT 9.7g (saturated fat 5.5g); PROTEIN 10g; CARBOHYDRATES 30.3g; FIBER 2.2g; CHOLESTEROL 16mg; IRON 2.2mg; SODIUM 547mg; CALCIUM 135mg

---

Menu
POINTS value
per serving: 5

Goat Cheese, Tomato, and Basil Pizza

1 cup garden salad with fat-free balsamic vinaigrette
POINTS value: 0

Game Plan

1. While oven preheats:
• Prepare pizza crust.

2. While pizza cooks:
• Prepare salad.

---

pictured on page 40

Southwestern Rice and Veggie Cakes

prep: 7 minutes • **cook:** 8 minutes   ***POINTS*** value: 7

Not only does the cheese add flavor to this dish, but it also helps hold the cakes together; the thicker the shred of cheese, the better.

  2 (1.5-ounce) slices double fiber bread
  2 (8.5-ounce) packages Santa Fe precooked whole-grain rice medley (such as Uncle Ben's Santa Fe Ready Rice)
  4 large egg whites, lightly beaten
  ¾ cup (3 ounces) preshredded reduced-fat 4-cheese Mexican blend cheese
     Cooking spray
  ½ cup reduced-fat sour cream
  2 teaspoons fresh lime juice
  ¼ teaspoon chili powder
     Chopped fresh cilantro (optional)

1. Place bread slices in a food processor, and pulse 10 times or until crumbs measure 1 cup. Combine crumbs, rice, egg whites, and cheese in a large bowl; mix well. Divide mixture into 8 equal portions, shaping each into a 2-inch patty.
2. Heat a large nonstick skillet over medium-high heat. Coat pan with cooking spray. Add 4 patties to pan; cook 3 minutes. Carefully turn patties over; cook 1 minute or until lightly browned. Repeat procedure with remaining 4 patties. While patties cook, combine sour cream, lime juice, and chili powder in a small bowl.
3. Arrange cakes on a serving platter. Top each with sour cream mixture. Garnish with cilantro, if desired. **Yield:** 4 servings (serving size: 2 rice cakes and 2 tablespoons sour cream mixture).

Per serving: CALORIES 349 (28% from fat); FAT 11g (saturated fat 3.8g); PROTEIN 19.2g; CARBOHYDRATES 47.7g; FIBER 7.3g; CHOLESTEROL 25mg; IRON 2.2mg; SODIUM 851mg; CALCIUM 321mg

Spicy Tricolor Bell Pepper Stir-Fry

prep: 4 minutes • **cook:** 5 minutes   ***POINTS*** value: 1

  2 teaspoons canola oil
  3 bell peppers (1 each of red, yellow, and green), cut into strips
  1 garlic clove, minced
  ¼ teaspoon crushed red pepper
  ¼ teaspoon salt

1. Heat oil in a large nonstick skillet over medium-high heat. Add peppers, garlic, and crushed red pepper. Stir-fry 4 minutes or until crisp-tender; sprinkle evenly with salt. **Yield:** 4 servings (serving size: ¾ cup).

Per serving: CALORIES 46 (53% from fat); FAT 3g (saturated fat 0.2g); PROTEIN 0.9g; CARBOHYDRATES 5.4g; FIBER 1.4g; CHOLESTEROL 0mg; IRON 0.4mg; SODIUM 148mg; CALCIUM 9mg

---

Menu
POINTS value
per serving: 8

Southwestern Rice and Veggie Cakes

Spicy Tricolor Bell Pepper Stir-Fry

Game Plan

1. Prepare bread crumbs.

2. Cut bell peppers into strips and mince garlic.

3. Shape rice mixture into patties.

4. While patties cook:
  • Prepare sour cream mixture.
  • Cook bell peppers.

Menu
POINTS value
per serving: 4

Grain and Vegetable–Stuffed Portobello Mushroom

Lemon Asparagus

Game Plan

1. While broiler preheats:
 • Remove mushroom gills, and mince garlic.

2. While mushrooms cook:
 • Prepare stuffing.

3. While stuffed mushrooms cook:
 • Trim and season asparagus; assemble on pan.

4. Cook asparagus.

Grain and Vegetable–Stuffed Portobello Mushrooms

prep: 5 minutes • **cook:** 7 minutes   *POINTS* value: 4

    4   (5-inch) portobello caps, gills removed
    Cooking spray
    1   garlic clove, minced
    1   cup refrigerated prechopped tomato, onion, and bell pepper mix
    1   (8.5-ounce) package precooked vegetable harvest whole-grain rice medley
        (such as Uncle Ben's Vegetable Harvest Ready Rice)
    1   cup (4 ounces) shredded Italian cheese blend, divided
    2   teaspoons Worcestershire sauce
    ¼   teaspoon salt
    ¼   teaspoon freshly ground black pepper

1. Preheat broiler.
2. Place mushrooms, gill sides down, on a foil-lined baking sheet coated with cooking spray. Broil 4 minutes.
3. While mushrooms broil, heat a nonstick skillet over medium heat. Coat pan with cooking spray. Add garlic and tomato mixture to pan. Sauté 2 minutes; remove from heat. Stir in rice, ¾ cup cheese, and Worcestershire sauce.
4. Turn mushrooms over; sprinkle evenly with salt and pepper. Divide rice mixture evenly among mushrooms; sprinkle evenly with ¼ cup cheese. Broil 3 minutes or until cheese melts. **Yield:** 4 servings (serving size: 1 stuffed mushroom).

Per serving: CALORIES 220 (31% from fat); FAT 8g (saturated fat 3.5g); PROTEIN 12g; CARBOHYDRATES 25.7g; FIBER 4g; CHOLESTEROL 20mg; IRON 1.4mg; SODIUM 681mg; CALCIUM 227mg

Lemon Asparagus

prep: 3 minutes • **cook:** 3 minutes   *POINTS* value: 0

    1   pound asparagus, trimmed
    1   garlic clove, minced
    ½   teaspoon grated fresh lemon rind
    ½   teaspoon olive oil
    ⅛   teaspoon salt
    ⅛   teaspoon freshly ground black pepper
    Cooking spray

1. Preheat broiler.
2. Combine all ingredients except cooking spray in a large bowl or dish; toss gently to coat.
3. Place asparagus on a foil-lined baking sheet coated with cooking spray. Broil 3 minutes. **Yield:** 4 servings (serving size: ¼ pound asparagus).

Per serving: CALORIES 21 (30% from fat); FAT 1g (saturated fat 0.1g); PROTEIN 1.4g; CARBOHYDRATES 2.7g; FIBER 1.3g; CHOLESTEROL 0mg; IRON 1.3mg; SODIUM 74mg; CALCIUM 16mg

Meats

pictured on page 44

Beef Tenderloin Steaks with Red Wine–Mushroom Sauce

prep: 1 minute • **cook:** 10 minutes   *POINTS* value: 5

Stirring the mushrooms constantly helps release their juices, allowing them to caramelize quickly. To cook the potatoes, microwave 4 (5-ounce) baked potatoes at HIGH 8 to 9 minutes or until tender, rearranging after 5 minutes. Wrap the potatoes in a towel, and let stand for 5 minutes before serving. For added color, try sprinkling chopped green onions on top of the potatoes.

  4 (4-ounce) beef tenderloin steaks, trimmed (about ½ inch thick)
  ¼ teaspoon salt
  ¼ teaspoon freshly ground black pepper
Butter-flavored cooking spray
  1 (8-ounce) package presliced baby portobello mushrooms
  1 cup dry red wine
  2 tablespoons butter
  1 teaspoon minced fresh rosemary
Fresh thyme sprigs (optional)

1. Heat a large nonstick skillet over medium-high heat. Sprinkle steaks with salt and pepper; coat with cooking spray. Add steaks to pan; cook 3 minutes on each side or until desired degree of doneness. Transfer steaks to a serving platter; keep warm.
2. Add mushrooms to pan. Coat mushrooms with cooking spray; sauté 3 minutes or until browned. Stir in wine, scraping pan to loosen browned bits. Cook until liquid almost evaporates. Remove pan from heat; add butter and rosemary, stirring until butter melts. Pour sauce over steaks. Garnish with thyme sprigs, if desired.
Yield: 4 servings (serving size: 1 steak and ¼ cup sauce).

Per serving: CALORIES 244 (46% from fat); FAT 13g (saturated fat 6g); PROTEIN 23.3g; CARBOHYDRATES 3.8g; FIBER 0.9g; CHOLESTEROL 74mg; IRON 1.9mg; SODIUM 235mg; CALCIUM 24mg

Menu
POINTS value
per serving: 8

Beef Tenderloin Steaks with Red Wine–Mushroom Sauce

1 (5-ounce) baked potato with
1 teaspoon butter and
1 tablespoon sour cream
POINTS value: 3

Game Plan

1. Cook potatoes in microwave, and let stand.

2. While potatoes cook:
• Prepare steaks.

Seared Beef Tenderloin Steaks with Dark Beer Reduction and Blue Cheese

prep: 2 minutes • **cook:** 8 minutes

POINTS value: 5

Dark beer sauce and piquant blue cheese elevate this dish to steak-house quality. Finish cooking the steaks in the oven after searing; place them on the same pan as the Garlic-Herb Steak Fries to save cleanup time.

    2   teaspoons steak seasoning (such as McCormick Grill Mates)
    4   (4-ounce) beef tenderloin steaks, trimmed (about 1 inch thick)
    1   teaspoon olive oil
    1   (12-ounce) bottle dark lager (such as Michelob AmberBock)
    2   tablespoons light brown sugar
    2   tablespoons crumbled blue cheese

1. Preheat oven to 450°.
2. Rub steak seasoning over both sides of steaks.
3. Heat olive oil in a large nonstick skillet over medium-high heat. Add steaks; cook 2 minutes on each side or until browned. Remove steaks from pan; place on a baking sheet. Bake at 450° for 4 to 5 minutes or until desired degree of doneness.
4. While steaks bake, combine beer and brown sugar in a medium bowl; add to pan, scraping pan to loosen browned bits. Cook 6 minutes or until mixture is slightly syrupy and reduced to about ¼ cup. Serve steaks with reduced sauce; sprinkle evenly with cheese. **Yield:** 4 servings (serving size: 1 steak, about 1½ tablespoons sauce, and 1½ teaspoons cheese).

Per serving: CALORIES 209 (37% from fat); FAT 8g (saturated fat 3.2g); PROTEIN 22.7g; CARBOHYDRATES 6.2g; FIBER 0g; CHOLESTEROL 62mg; IRON 1.5mg; SODIUM 362mg; CALCIUM 37mg

Garlic-Herb Steak Fries

prep: 4 minutes • **cook:** 17 minutes

POINTS value: 3

    3   cups (15 ounces) frozen steak fries
    1   tablespoon chopped fresh rosemary
    1   tablespoon olive oil
    1   teaspoon garlic–sea salt blend (such as McCormick)

1. Preheat oven to 450°.
2. Combine all ingredients in a large bowl. Arrange fries in a single layer on a large baking sheet. Bake at 450° for 17 minutes or until lightly browned, stirring once. **Yield:** 4 servings (serving size: about ¾ cup).

Per serving: CALORIES 170 (38% from fat); FAT 7g (saturated fat 2.4g); PROTEIN 2.6g; CARBOHYDRATES 24.2g; FIBER 2.6g; CHOLESTEROL 0mg; IRON 0.5mg; SODIUM 489mg; CALCIUM 2mg

---

Menu
POINTS value
per serving: 8

Seared Beef Tenderloin Steaks with Dark Beer Reduction and Blue Cheese

Garlic-Herb Steak Fries

Game Plan

1. While oven preheats:
  • Combine ingredients for steak fries; assemble fries on pan.

2. While steak fries cook:
  • Sear steaks; bake steaks on pan with fries.
  • Prepare sauce.

3. Top steaks with cheese.

pictured on page 42

Sweet-and-Spicy Sirloin Steak

prep: 4 minutes • **cook:** 8 minutes • **other:** 10 minutes   ***POINTS*** value: 4

Menu
POINTS value
per serving: 4

Sweet-and-Spicy
Sirloin Steak

1 cup grilled asparagus
POINTS value: 0

Game Plan

1. While grill heats:
   • Marinate steak.
   • Trim asparagus.

2. Grill steak and asparagus.

3. Prepare sauce.

Chili sauce with garlic is a common Asian condiment made from blended fresh chilies. We've used a small amount here for a hint of heat, but if you're a fan of spicy foods, add more for an extra punch. To make this dish ahead, marinate the steaks in the refrigerator overnight. For heartier fare, serve with ½ cup microwavable precooked rice for a meal with a *POINTS* value of 6.

    ¼ cup less-sodium soy sauce (such as Kikkoman)
    2 tablespoons sugar
    2 tablespoons balsamic vinegar
    1 teaspoon chili sauce with garlic (such as Hokan)
    1 pound boneless sirloin steak (¾ inch thick)
    Cooking spray

1. Prepare grill.
2. Combine first 4 ingredients in a small bowl, stirring with a whisk. Reserve 2 tablespoons marinade, and place in a small microwave-safe bowl. Cover and set aside.
3. Place steak in a large heavy-duty zip-top plastic bag. Add remaining marinade to bag; seal well. Marinate 10 minutes, turning occasionally.
4. Remove steak from marinade, discarding marinade. Place steak on grill rack coated with cooking spray. Grill 4 to 5 minutes on each side or to desired degree of doneness. Transfer steak to a cutting board; cut steak into thin slices.
5. While steak marinates, microwave reserved marinade at HIGH 45 seconds or until thoroughly heated; drizzle over steak. **Yield:** 4 servings (serving size: 3 ounces steak and 1½ teaspoons sauce).

Per serving: CALORIES 176 (24% from fat); FAT 4.6g (saturated fat 1.8g); PROTEIN 25g; CARBOHYDRATES 6.6g; FIBER 0g; CHOLESTEROL 46mg; IRON 1.7mg; SODIUM 366mg; CALCIUM 19mg

Flank Steak with Herb Spread

prep: 3 minutes • **cook:** 12 minutes • **other:** 5 minutes   *POINTS* value: 5

- 1 lemon
- 1 (1-pound) flank steak, trimmed
- 3 large garlic cloves, minced and divided
- ½ teaspoon salt, divided
- ¼ teaspoon freshly ground black pepper
- Cooking spray
- ¼ cup yogurt-based spread (such as Brummel & Brown)
- 1 tablespoon chopped fresh parsley
- 1 teaspoon chopped fresh rosemary

1. Prepare grill.

2. Grate rind and squeeze juice from lemon to measure 2 teaspoons rind and 2 tablespoons juice. Drizzle flank steak with lemon juice and sprinkle with 1 minced garlic clove, rubbing juice and garlic into steak. Sprinkle steak with ¼ teaspoon salt and pepper. Place steak on grill rack coated with cooking spray; grill 6 minutes on each side or until desired degree of doneness. Transfer steak to a cutting board; let stand 5 minutes. Cut steak diagonally across grain into thin slices.

3. While steak stands, combine yogurt-based spread, lemon rind, 2 minced garlic cloves, ¼ teaspoon salt, parsley, and rosemary, stirring until blended. Serve over steak. **Yield:** 4 servings (serving size: 3 ounces steak and 1 tablespoon herb mixture).

Per serving: CALORIES 211 (48% from fat); FAT 11.2g (saturated fat 3.3g); PROTEIN 24.8g; CARBOHYDRATES 1.7g; FIBER 0.3g; CHOLESTEROL 37mg; IRON 1.9mg; SODIUM 444mg; CALCIUM 35mg

Grilled Asparagus and Tomatoes

prep: 2 minutes • **cook:** 6 minutes   *POINTS* value: 1

- 1 pound fresh asparagus, trimmed
- 4 plum tomatoes, halved
- 1 tablespoon olive oil
- Cooking spray
- ¼ teaspoon salt
- ⅛ teaspoon black pepper
- ½ teaspoon grated fresh lemon rind

1. Prepare grill.

2. Place asparagus and tomato halves in an 11 x 7–inch baking dish. Drizzle vegetables with oil; toss gently to coat. Place vegetables on grill rack coated with cooking spray. Grill asparagus 3 minutes on each side; grill tomato 1 minute on each side. Return asparagus and tomato to dish. Sprinkle vegetables with salt, pepper, and lemon rind. **Yield:** 4 servings (serving size: ¼ of asparagus and 2 tomato halves).

Per serving: CALORIES 62 (54% from fat); FAT 3.7g (saturated fat 0.5g); PROTEIN 3.8g; CARBOHYDRATES 5.7g; FIBER 1.3g; CHOLESTEROL 0mg; IRON 0.9mg; SODIUM 151mg; CALCIUM 27mg

---

Menu
POINTS value
per serving: 6

**Flank Steak
with Herb Spread**

**Grilled Asparagus
and Tomatoes**

Game Plan

1. While grill heats:
- Trim asparagus, and halve tomatoes.
- Season asparagus and tomatoes; assemble in pan.
- Zest and juice lemon.
- Season steak.

2. Grill steak and tomatoes.

3. While steak stands:
- Prepare herbed butter.

meats **73**

Menu
POINTS value
per serving: 8

Mongolian Beef

½ cup precooked rice
POINTS value: 2

Game Plan

1. Cut flank steak, and toss with cornstarch.

2. Prepare water mixture.

3. While steak mixture cooks:
• Microwave rice.

Mongolian Beef

prep: 6 minutes • **cook:** 9 minutes **POINTS** value: 6

For a filling addition to this meal, serve with 1 cup steamed broccoli or sugar snap peas for an additional *POINTS* value of 0 per serving.

1 pound flank steak, trimmed
1½ tablespoons cornstarch
½ cup water
⅓ cup firmly packed brown sugar
⅓ cup less-sodium soy sauce (such as Kikkoman)
1 tablespoon canola oil
3 garlic cloves, minced
½ teaspoon grated peeled fresh ginger
¼ cup sliced green onions

1. Cut steak diagonally across grain into thin slices. Combine steak and cornstarch in a medium bowl; toss until coated, and set aside.
2. Combine water, brown sugar, and soy sauce in a small bowl; set aside.
3. Heat oil in a large nonstick skillet over medium-high heat. Add garlic and ginger; sauté 1 minute. Add steak; cook 3 minutes or until browned, stirring occasionally. Add brown sugar mixture, and cook 4 minutes or until sauce thickens, stirring occasionally. Sprinkle with green onions. **Yield:** 4 servings (serving size: ⅔ cup beef mixture).

Per serving: CALORIES 285 (29% from fat); FAT 9.2g (saturated fat 2.6g); PROTEIN 25.9g; CARBOHYDRATES 23.1g; FIBER 0.3g; CHOLESTEROL 39mg; IRON 2mg; SODIUM 865mg; CALCIUM 47mg

Chili-Rubbed Sirloin Steak

prep: 3 minutes • **cook:** 11 minutes • **other:** 5 minutes   ***POINTS*** value: 4

     1   pound boneless sirloin steak (1 inch thick)
    1½   tablespoons chili seasoning (such as French's)
     ¼   teaspoon freshly ground black pepper
         Cooking spray
     ½   cup water
     1   tablespoon balsamic vinegar
     1   teaspoon instant coffee granules
    1½   teaspoons Worcestershire sauce
     ¼   teaspoon salt

1. Sprinkle both sides of steak with chili seasoning and pepper; firmly press spices into steak. Coat steak with cooking spray.
2. Heat a large nonstick skillet over medium-high heat. Add steak, and cook 4 minutes. Reduce heat to medium; turn steak, and cook 4 minutes or until desired degree of doneness. Transfer steak to a cutting board; let stand 5 minutes.
3. While steak cooks, combine ½ cup water and next 4 ingredients in a small bowl, stirring well with a whisk.
4. Reheat pan over medium-high heat; add vinegar mixture to pan. Cook until liquid is reduced to ¼ cup, scraping pan to loosen browned bits.
5. Cut steak into thin slices, and drizzle with sauce. **Yield:** 4 servings (serving size: 3 ounces steak and 1 tablespoon sauce).

Per serving: CALORIES 160 (26% from fat); FAT 4.7g (saturated fat 1.8g); PROTEIN 24.6g; CARBOHYDRATES 2.7g; FIBER 0g; CHOLESTEROL 46mg; IRON 1.7mg; SODIUM 307mg; CALCIUM 20mg

Mini Cheddar Potato Skins

prep: 5 minutes • **cook:** 6 minutes • **other:** 5 minutes   ***POINTS*** value: 3

     1   pound red fingerling potatoes (about 20)
     1   tablespoon butter, melted
     ¼   teaspoon salt
     ¼   teaspoon black pepper
     3   tablespoons reduced-fat shredded extra-sharp Cheddar cheese
     2   tablespoons thinly sliced green onions

1. Place potatoes in a single layer in a microwave-safe bowl (do not pierce potatoes with a fork). Cover bowl with plastic wrap (do not allow plastic wrap to touch food); vent. Microwave at HIGH 5 to 6 minutes or until tender. Let stand 5 minutes or until cool enough to touch. Cut potatoes in half; drizzle evenly with butter, and sprinkle evenly with salt and pepper. Top evenly with cheese. Microwave at HIGH 30 seconds or until cheese melts. Sprinkle evenly with green onions. **Yield:** 4 servings (serving size: about 5 potato halves).

Per serving: CALORIES 149 (23% from fat); FAT 4.2g (saturated fat 2.6g); PROTEIN 3.9g; CARBOHYDRATES 24.4g; FIBER 2.5g; CHOLESTEROL 12mg; IRON 0.8mg; SODIUM 174mg; CALCIUM 55mg

Menu
POINTS value
per serving: 7

Chili-Rubbed Sirloin Steak

Mini Cheddar Potato Skins

Game Plan

1. While potatoes cook in microwave and stand:
• Cook steaks.
• Combine ingredients for sauce.
• Slice green onions.

2. While steak stands:
• Cook sauce.
• Microwave cheese-topped potato skins.

Menu
POINTS value
per serving: 8

Beef, Bell Pepper, and Asparagus with Hoisin Sauce

½ cup cooked rice noodles
POINTS value: 2

Game Plan

1. While water for rice noodles comes to a boil:
- Slice bell pepper and onion.
- Cut asparagus.
- Cut flank steak.
- Prepare beef mixture and chicken broth mixture.

2. While noodles soak according to package directions:
- Prepare beef and vegetable stir-fry mixture.

Beef, Bell Pepper, and Asparagus with Hoisin Sauce

prep: 8 minutes • **cook:** 9 minutes

POINTS value: 6

For a variation, try serving this saucy beef stir-fry over ½ cup cooked rice for a meal with a *POINTS* value of 8 per serving.

- 2 tablespoons less-sodium soy sauce, divided
- 2 tablespoons cornstarch, divided
- 1 pound boneless sirloin steak, cut into ½-inch strips
- ½ cup fat-free, less-sodium chicken broth
- 2 tablespoons hoisin sauce
- 1 tablespoon rice vinegar
- 1 teaspoon dark sesame oil
- ¼ teaspoon crushed red pepper
- 4 teaspoons canola oil, divided
- 1 yellow bell pepper, thinly sliced
- 1 pound asparagus, trimmed and cut into 2-inch pieces
- 1 green onion, thinly sliced

1. Combine 1 tablespoon soy sauce and 1 tablespoon cornstarch in a medium bowl, stirring with a whisk until smooth. Add beef, and toss to coat.

2. Combine remaining 1 tablespoon soy sauce, remaining 1 tablespoon cornstarch, chicken broth, and next 4 ingredients in a small bowl; stir with a whisk.

3. Heat 2 teaspoons canola oil in a large nonstick skillet over medium-high heat. Add beef to pan, and sauté 5 minutes or until lightly browned. Remove beef from pan, and set aside. Add remaining 2 teaspoons canola oil to pan.

4. Add bell pepper and asparagus; sauté 3 minutes or just until crisp-tender. Stir in beef and chicken broth mixture; cook, stirring constantly, 30 seconds or until sauce thickens. Sprinkle with green onions. **Yield:** 6 servings (serving size: about ¾ cup).

Per serving: CALORIES 243 (54% from fat); FAT 14.6g (saturated fat 4.5g); PROTEIN 17.3g; CARBOHYDRATES 10.6g; FIBER 2g; CHOLESTEROL 51mg; IRON 2.3mg; SODIUM 375mg; CALCIUM 27mg

Beef, Mushroom, and Tomato Ragu

prep: 3 minutes • **cook:** 17 minutes

POINTS value: 7

Ragu is a meat sauce that is a staple in Northern Italian cuisine. We suggest serving this robust sauce over cooked orzo, but you may use any type of pasta you like. When boiling the water for the pasta, start with hot water, and cover the pot tightly with a lid to speed up the process.

Olive oil–flavored cooking spray
¾ pound 93% lean ground beef
¼ teaspoon freshly ground black pepper
2 (8-ounce) packages presliced baby portobello mushrooms
1 cup prechopped onion
2 garlic cloves, minced
2 (14.5-ounce) cans diced tomatoes with basil, garlic, and oregano, undrained
½ cup fat-free, less-sodium chicken broth
¼ cup tomato paste
½ teaspoon dried Italian seasoning
3 cups hot cooked orzo (about 1¼ cups uncooked rice-shaped pasta)
6 tablespoons grated fresh Parmesan cheese

1. Heat a large nonstick skillet over medium-high heat. Coat pan with cooking spray. Add beef and pepper; cook 3 to 4 minutes or until browned, stirring to crumble. Add mushrooms and onion, and cook 4 minutes or until tender, stirring frequently. Add garlic, and cook 1 minute or until tender. Add diced tomatoes and next 3 ingredients; bring to a boil. Reduce heat; simmer, uncovered, 6 minutes or until slightly thick.

2. Spoon meat sauce over cooked orzo, and top each serving with cheese.

Yield: 6 servings (serving size: ½ cup orzo, about 1 cup meat sauce, and 1 tablespoon Parmesan cheese).

Per serving: CALORIES 337 (16% from fat); FAT 6.1g (saturated fat 2.6g); PROTEIN 22.2g; CARBOHYDRATES 48.5g; FIBER 3.7g; CHOLESTEROL 32mg; IRON 5.3mg; SODIUM 955mg; CALCIUM 175mg

Menu
POINTS value
per serving: 7

Beef, Mushroom, and Tomato Ragu

1 cup steamed zucchini spears
POINTS value: 0

Game Plan

1. While water for pasta comes to a boil:
• Prepare meat mixture.

2. While pasta cooks:
• Simmer meat sauce.
• Steam zucchini.

Menu

POINTS value
per serving: 8

Salisbury Steak

½ cup refrigerated
mashed potatoes
POINTS value: 2

1 cup garden salad with
fat-free red-wine vinaigrette
POINTS value: 0

Game Plan

1. While mushrooms cook:
• Open cans of consommé
and soup.

2. While sauce simmers:
• Shape and cook patties.

3. While sauce and patties cook:
• Microwave potatoes.
• Assemble salad.
• Combine remaining
consommé and cornstarch.

4. Add consommé-cornstarch
mixture to sauce; boil.

Salisbury Steak

prep: 1 minute • **cook:** 19 minutes

POINTS value: 6

Cooking the mushroom sauce and patties at the same time in separate skillets speeds up the preparation of this traditionally slow-cooked dish.

Cooking spray
1   (8-ounce) package presliced mushrooms
1   (10½-ounce) can beef consommé, divided
1   (10¾-ounce) can golden mushroom soup
½   teaspoon black pepper
⅓   cup dry breadcrumbs
1½ pounds ground round
2   large egg whites
½   cup prechopped onion
2   teaspoons cornstarch

1. Heat a large nonstick skillet over medium-high heat. Coat pan with cooking spray. Add mushrooms to pan; sauté over medium-high heat 2 minutes. Add beef consommé, reserving 1 tablespoon. Add mushroom soup and pepper; stir well to combine. Bring mixture to a boil; reduce heat, cover, and simmer.
2. While sauce simmers, combine breadcrumbs, beef, egg whites, and onion in a bowl. Shape into 6 (½-inch-thick) patties.
3. Heat a large nonstick skillet over medium-high heat; coat pan with cooking spray. Add patties; cook 3 to 4 minutes on each side or until browned. Transfer mushroom sauce to pan with patties. Cook 5 to 6 minutes or until meat is done.
4. Combine reserved 1 tablespoon consommé and cornstarch in a small bowl, stirring with a whisk; add to pan. Bring to a boil; cook 1 minute or until thick.
Yield: 6 servings (serving size: 1 patty and ⅓ cup sauce).

Per serving: CALORIES 275 (43% from fat); FAT 13.1g (saturated fat 5g); PROTEIN 28.6g; CARBOHYDRATES 10.1g; FIBER 1.5g; CHOLESTEROL 76mg; IRON 3.3mg; SODIUM 740mg; CALCIUM 28mg

Shepherd's Pie

prep: 2 minutes • **cook:** 13 minutes   ***POINTS*** value: 6

Look for pretrimmed green beans in convenient microwave-safe packaging in the produce section of your supermarket.

¾	pound 93% lean ground beef
1	(14.5-ounce) can diced tomatoes with basil, garlic, and oregano, undrained
1	(8-ounce) can no-salt-added tomato sauce
1½	cups frozen baby vegetable mix (such as Birds Eye)
2	cups country-style refrigerated mashed potatoes (such as Simply Potatoes)
	Cooking spray
⅛	teaspoon freshly ground black pepper

1. Preheat broiler.

2. Cook beef in a large nonstick skillet over medium-high heat until browned, stirring to crumble. Add tomatoes, tomato sauce, and vegetable mix. Cook 5 minutes or until mixture is slightly thick and thoroughly heated, stirring occasionally.

3. While beef mixture cooks, place potatoes in a microwave-safe bowl. Cover with plastic wrap; vent. Microwave at HIGH 2 minutes or until thoroughly heated.

4. Spoon beef mixture evenly into each of 4 (8-ounce) broiler-safe ramekins coated with cooking spray. Top evenly with potatoes; sprinkle with pepper. Place ramekins on a baking sheet. Broil 2 to 3 minutes or until potatoes are golden.

Yield: 4 servings (serving size: 1 pie).

Per serving: CALORIES 320 (27% from fat); FAT 9.6g (saturated fat 4.8g); PROTEIN 20.4g; CARBOHYDRATES 36.5g; FIBER 4.7g; CHOLESTEROL 51mg; IRON 4.7mg; SODIUM 771mg; CALCIUM 103mg

---

Menu
POINTS value
per serving: 6

Shepherd's Pie

1 cup steamed green beans
POINTS value: 0

Game Plan

1. While broiler preheats:
- Prepare beef mixture.
- Microwave potatoes.

2. While ramekins broil:
- Steam green beans according to package directions.

pictured on page 43

Taco Salad Pizza

prep: 3 minutes • **cook:** 14 minutes   ***POINTS*** value: 8

Family favorite taco salad ingredients find their way onto a crisp prebaked pizza. Store remaining taco seasoning in a zip-top plastic storage bag or small airtight container.

<table>
<tr><td>8</td><td>ounces ground sirloin</td></tr>
<tr><td>1</td><td>(1-ounce) package 40%-less-sodium taco seasoning (such as Old El Paso)</td></tr>
<tr><td>¼</td><td>teaspoon freshly ground black pepper</td></tr>
<tr><td>⅔</td><td>cup water</td></tr>
<tr><td>1</td><td>(10-ounce) Italian cheese-flavored thin pizza crust (such as Boboli)</td></tr>
<tr><td colspan="2">Cooking spray</td></tr>
<tr><td>⅓</td><td>cup light sour cream</td></tr>
<tr><td>1</td><td>cup (4 ounces) reduced-fat shredded sharp Cheddar cheese</td></tr>
<tr><td>2</td><td>cups shredded iceberg lettuce</td></tr>
<tr><td>¾</td><td>cup grape tomatoes, halved</td></tr>
<tr><td>¼</td><td>cup sliced ripe olives</td></tr>
<tr><td colspan="2">Salsa (optional)</td></tr>
</table>

1. Preheat oven to 450°.

2. Brown beef in a large nonstick skillet over medium-high heat, stirring until it crumbles. Stir in 1½ teaspoons taco seasoning, reserving remaining seasoning for another use. Stir in pepper and ⅔ cup water. Bring to a boil; reduce heat, and simmer, uncovered, 2 minutes or until liquid is almost absorbed.

3. While meat mixture cooks, coat pizza crust with cooking spray. Place crust directly on center oven rack. Bake at 450° for 7 to 8 minutes or until browned. Quickly spread sour cream over crust to within 1 inch of edge. Sprinkle with meat mixture and cheese. Bake an additional 30 seconds or until cheese melts.

4. Remove pizza from oven; top with lettuce, tomato, and olives. Cut into 4 wedges. Serve with salsa, if desired. **Yield:** 4 servings (serving size: 1 wedge).

Per serving: CALORIES 394 (33% from fat); FAT 14.6g (saturated fat 6.9g); PROTEIN 28.4g; CARBOHYDRATES 41.8g; FIBER 6.3g; CHOLESTEROL 57mg; IRON 3.2mg; SODIUM 811mg; CALCIUM 320mg

---

Menu
POINTS value
per serving: 8

Taco Salad Pizza

Game Plan

1. While oven preheats:
- Halve tomatoes; measure lettuce, cheese, and olives.

2. While meat mixture cooks:
- Bake crust.

3. Top crust with sour cream, meat mixture, and cheese; bake.

4. Top pizza with remaining salad toppings.

Lemon-Caper Pork Medallions

prep: 5 minutes • **cook:** 9 minutes   ***POINTS*** value: 4

This simple lemon-caper sauce would also be delicious served with chicken or fish.

 1   (1-pound) pork tenderloin, trimmed
 ½   teaspoon freshly ground black pepper
 ¼   teaspoon salt
 1   tablespoon olive oil
 ¾   cup fat-free, less-sodium chicken broth
 3   tablespoons capers
 2   tablespoons fresh lemon juice
 1   lemon, thinly sliced

1. Cut tenderloin crosswise into 8 slices; place between 2 sheets of plastic wrap, and pound to ¼-inch thickness using a meat mallet or small heavy skillet. Sprinkle pork with pepper and salt. Heat oil in a large nonstick skillet over medium-high heat. Add pork, and cook 2 minutes on each side or until browned.
2. Add broth and remaining ingredients to pan; bring to a boil. Cook 2 to 3 minutes or until liquid is reduced by half. Transfer pork to a serving platter. Spoon sauce and lemon slices over pork medallions. **Yield:** 4 servings (serving size: 3 ounces pork and 2 tablespoons sauce).

Per serving: CALORIES 168 (40% from fat); FAT 7.4g (saturated fat 1.8g); PROTEIN 23.3g; CARBOHYDRATES 1.3g; FIBER 0.3g; CHOLESTEROL 63mg; IRON 1.3mg; SODIUM 488mg; CALCIUM 9mg

Herbed-Buttered Angel Hair Pasta

prep: 3 minutes • **cook:** 10 minutes   ***POINTS*** value: 3

 4   ounces angel hair pasta
 1   tablespoon butter
 2   teaspoons chopped fresh parsley
 ¼   teaspoon salt
 ⅛   teaspoon freshly ground black pepper

1. Cook pasta according to package directions, omitting salt and fat.
2. Combine cooked pasta, butter, parsley, salt, and pepper; toss gently. Serve immediately. **Yield:** 4 servings (serving size: ½ cup).

Per serving: CALORIES 127 (25% from fat); FAT 3.5g (saturated fat 2g); PROTEIN 3.8g; CARBOHYDRATES 20.7g; FIBER 1g; CHOLESTEROL 8mg; IRON 1mg; SODIUM 167mg; CALCIUM 8mg

---

Menu
POINTS value
per serving: 7

Lemon-Caper Pork Medallions

Herbed-Buttered Angel Hair Pasta

Game Plan

1. While water for pasta comes to a boil:
 • Juice and slice lemons.
 • Chop parsley.
 • Cut, pound, and season pork.

2. While pasta cooks:
 • Cook pork and sauce.

Menu
POINTS value
per serving: 5

Orange-Hoisin Pork Tenderloin

Edamame and
Roasted Red Bell Pepper Salad

Game Plan

1. Prepare salad.

2. Cut, pound, and season pork.

3. While pork cooks:
- Prepare sugar mixture.
- Cook sauce.

Orange-Hoisin Pork Tenderloin

prep: 3 minutes • **cook:** 12 minutes   ***POINTS*** value: 3

You will enjoy the tantalizing aroma as you prepare this colorful meal. Pounding the pork slices ensures a fork-tender bite.

  1 (1-pound) pork tenderloin, trimmed
  ½ teaspoon coarsely ground black pepper
  ¼ teaspoon salt
  Cooking spray
  1 tablespoon sugar
  1 tablespoon less-sodium soy sauce (such as Kikkoman)
  1 tablespoon water
  1 tablespoon hoisin sauce
  2 teaspoons grated fresh orange rind
  2 teaspoons cider vinegar

1. Cut pork crosswise into ¾-inch-thick slices; place between 2 sheets of plastic wrap and pound to ½-inch thickness with a meat mallet or small heavy skillet. Sprinkle pork with pepper and salt.
2. Heat a large nonstick skillet over medium-high heat. Coat pan with cooking spray. Add pork to pan in batches; cook 3 minutes on each side or until done.
3. While pork cooks, combine sugar and next 5 ingredients in a small bowl.
4. Remove pork from pan; place on a serving platter. Add sugar mixture to pan, scraping pan to loosen browned bits. Pour sauce over pork. **Yield:** 4 servings (serving size: 3 ounces pork and 1½ teaspoons sauce).

Per serving: CALORIES 154 (19% from fat); FAT 3.2g (saturated fat 0.9g); PROTEIN 24.1g; CARBOHYDRATES 5.5g; FIBER 0.2g; CHOLESTEROL 74mg; IRON 1.1mg; SODIUM 415mg; CALCIUM 8mg

Edamame and Roasted Red Bell Pepper Salad

prep: 5 minutes   ***POINTS*** value: 2

  1 cup chopped bottled roasted red bell peppers
  ¼ cup chopped fresh cilantro
  2 tablespoons sesame ginger dressing (such as Newman's Own)
  1 tablespoon minced peeled fresh ginger
  1 (10-ounce) package refrigerated ready-to-eat shelled edamame (such as Marjon)

1. Combine all ingredients in a medium bowl; toss to coat. **Yield:** 4 servings (serving size: about ⅔ cup).

Per serving: CALORIES 123 (27% from fat); FAT 3.7g (saturated fat 0.1g); PROTEIN 8.4g; CARBOHYDRATES 13.1g; FIBER 4.2g; CHOLESTEROL 0mg; IRON 2mg; SODIUM 333mg; CALCIUM 54mg

pictured on page 46

Pork Medallions with Sherry Glaze

prep: 2 minutes • **cook:** 11 minutes   **POINTS** value: 4

Combine just three simple ingredients to make this elegant, dark sauce for the tender slices of pork.

Cooking spray
1   (1-pound) pork tenderloin, trimmed and cut into ¾-inch-thick slices
½   teaspoon salt
¼   teaspoon freshly ground black pepper
6   tablespoons dry sherry
¼   cup sherry vinegar
2   tablespoons brown sugar

1. Heat a large nonstick skillet over medium-high heat. Coat pan with cooking spray. Sprinkle pork evenly with salt and pepper. Add pork to pan in batches; cook 2 to 3 minutes on each side or until done. Remove pork from pan; keep warm.
2. While pork cooks, combine sherry, vinegar, and brown sugar in a small bowl, stirring with a whisk; set aside.
3. Add sherry mixture to pan, scraping pan to loosen browned bits. Bring to a boil; cook 1 minute or until thick and reduced to ⅓ cup sauce. Return pork to pan, turning to coat with sauce. **Yield:** 4 servings (serving size: 3 ounces pork and 1 tablespoon sauce).

Per serving: CALORIES 166 (14% from fat); FAT 2.5g (saturated fat 0.8g); PROTEIN 23.8g; CARBOHYDRATES 8.8g; FIBER 0g; CHOLESTEROL 74mg; IRON 1.2mg; SODIUM 493mg; CALCIUM 13mg

Arugula-Strawberry Salad

prep: 7 minutes   **POINTS** value: 1

2   tablespoons fresh lemon juice
1   tablespoon honey
2   teaspoons olive oil
¼   teaspoon kosher salt
¼   teaspoon freshly ground black pepper
4   cups packed arugula
2   cups strawberries, sliced

1. Combine first 5 ingredients in a large bowl, stirring with a whisk. Add arugula and strawberries; toss well. **Yield:** 4 servings (serving size: about 1½ cups).

Per serving: CALORIES 70 (33% from fat); FAT 2.6g (saturated fat 0.3g); PROTEIN 1.1g; CARBOHYDRATES 12.2g; FIBER 2.1g; CHOLESTEROL 0mg; IRON 0.7mg; SODIUM 127mg; CALCIUM 47mg

---

Menu
POINTS value
per serving: 5

Pork Medallions with Sherry Glaze

Arugula-Strawberry Salad

Game Plan

1. Slice strawberries and prepare dressing for salad.

2. Cut and season pork.

3. While pork cooks:
• Combine ingredients for sherry mixture.

4. Cook sauce.

5. Toss salad.

Menu
POINTS value
per serving: 5

Pork with Chimichurri

Yellow Rice with Spring Peas

Game Plan

1. While onion cooks:
- Prepare and measure ingredients for chimichurri.

2. While rice cooks:
- Cook pork.
- Prepare chimichurri.

3. Add peas to rice.

Pork with Chimichurri

prep: 5 minutes • **cook:** 7 minutes   *POINTS* value: 4

Cooking spray
 4 (4-ounce) boneless loin pork chops (about ½ inch thick)
 ¼ teaspoon salt
 ¼ teaspoon black pepper
 2 garlic cloves
 1 large shallot, halved
 1 cup fresh flat-leaf parsley leaves
 ¼ cup fresh mint leaves
 1 tablespoon fresh lemon juice
 2 teaspoons olive oil

1. Heat a large nonstick skillet over medium-high heat; coat pan with cooking spray.
2. Sprinkle pork chops with salt and pepper. Add pork chops to pan; cook 4 minutes. Turn pork chops; cover and cook 3 minutes.
3. While pork chops cook, drop garlic and shallot through food chute with food processor on; process until minced. Add parsley, mint, lemon juice, and oil to food processor; process until mixture is finely chopped. Serve pork chops with chimichurri sauce. **Yield:** 4 servings (serving size: 1 pork chop and 2 tablespoons sauce).

Per serving: CALORIES 176 (42% from fat); FAT 8.2g (saturated fat 2g); PROTEIN 21.9g; CARBOHYDRATES 3g; FIBER 0.7g; CHOLESTEROL 66mg; IRON 1.8mg; SODIUM 202mg; CALCIUM 48mg

Yellow Rice with Spring Peas

prep: 1 minute • **cook:** 19 minutes   *POINTS* value: 1

Cooking spray
 ½ cup prechopped onion
 1 (3½-ounce) bag boil-in-bag long-grain rice
 ½ teaspoon ground turmeric
 ¾ cup fat-free, less-sodium chicken broth
 ½ cup water
 ⅛ teaspoon salt
 ½ cup frozen petite green peas

1. Heat a large nonstick skillet over medium-high heat. Coat pan with cooking spray. Add onion to pan; sauté 4 minutes or until tender. Cut open rice bag; pour rice into pan. Add turmeric; sauté 2 minutes. Add broth, ½ cup water, and salt; bring to a boil. Cover, reduce heat, and simmer 12 minutes or until rice is tender and liquid is absorbed. Stir in peas. **Yield:** 4 servings (serving size: ½ cup).

CALORIES 54 (1% from fat); FAT 0g (saturated fat 0g); PROTEIN 2.2g; CARBOHYDRATES 10.9g; FIBER 1.3g; CHOLESTEROL 0mg; IRON 0.6mg; SODIUM 219mg; CALCIUM 5mg

Five-Spice Pork with Apricots

prep: 8 minutes • **cook:** 8 minutes   *POINTS* value: 6

Five-spice powder is mostly used in Chinese cooking and incorporates the five basic flavors of cooking—sweet, sour, bitter, savory, and salty. Serve this tasty pork dish over rice.

    2   teaspoons dark sesame oil, divided
    Cooking spray
    1   pound boneless center-cut loin pork chops, cut into strips
    1½ teaspoons five-spice powder
    ¼   teaspoon salt
    1   bunch green onions, cut into 2-inch pieces
    ½   cup thinly sliced dried apricots
    2   teaspoons grated fresh orange rind
    1½ teaspoons sugar
    ¼   cup fresh orange juice

1. Heat 1 teaspoon oil in a large nonstick skillet coated with cooking spray over medium-high heat. Add pork; sprinkle with five-spice powder and salt. Cook 3 to 4 minutes or until pork loses its pink color. Remove from pan; keep warm.
2. Coat pan with cooking spray. Add remaining 1 teaspoon oil and green onions; sauté 2 minutes or until lightly browned. Return pork to pan, and stir in apricots, orange rind, and sugar. Cook 1 minute, stirring constantly. Remove pork mixture from pan; keep warm. Add orange juice to pan, scraping pan to loosen browned bits. Cook 1 minute or until syrupy. Drizzle reduced orange juice over pork mixture. Serve immediately. **Yield:** 4 servings (serving size: about ¾ cup pork mixture).

Per serving: CALORIES 258 (31% from fat); FAT 9g (saturated fat 2.7g); PROTEIN 25.2g; CARBOHYDRATES 18.4g; FIBER 1.8g; CHOLESTEROL 65mg; IRON 2.3mg; SODIUM 197mg; CALCIUM 62mg

Menu
POINTS value
per serving: 8

Five-Spice Pork with Apricots

½ cup precooked rice
POINTS value: 2

Game Plan

1. Cut green onions; slice apricots.

2. While pork cooks:
   • Zest and juice orange.
   • Microwave rice.

3. Cook sauce.

pictured on page 45

Parmesan-Crusted Pork Chops

Menu
POINTS value
per serving: 7

**Parmesan-Crusted
Pork Chops**

**Roasted Green Beans
with Prosciutto**

Game Plan

1. While oven preheats:
- Assemble green bean mixture on pan.

2. While green bean dish cooks:
- Pound pork; dredge in egg white and panko mixture.
- Cook pork.

prep: 5 minutes • **cook:** 7 minutes

POINTS value: 6

Parmesan cheese and crunchy breadcrumbs form a delicate crust on these fork-tender pork chops.

- 4 (4-ounce) boneless center-cut loin pork chops (about ½ inch thick)
- 1 egg white, lightly beaten
- ½ cup panko (Japanese breadcrumbs)
- ¼ cup (1 ounce) grated Parmesan cheese
- ¼ teaspoon salt
- ¼ teaspoon black pepper
- 1 tablespoon extra-virgin olive oil
- 4 lemon wedges
- 2 teaspoons chopped fresh thyme

1. Place pork between 2 sheets of plastic wrap; pound to an even thickness (about ¼ inch) using a meat mallet or small heavy skillet.
2. Place egg white in a shallow dish. Combine panko, cheese, salt, and pepper in a shallow dish. Dip pork in egg white; dredge in panko mixture, pressing gently with fingers to coat.
3. Heat oil in a large nonstick skillet over medium heat. Add pork; cook 3 to 4 minutes on each side or until lightly browned. Squeeze 1 lemon wedge over each pork chop; sprinkle evenly with thyme. **Yield:** 4 servings (serving size: 1 pork chop).

Per serving: CALORIES 253 (44% from fat); FAT 12g (saturated fat 4.1g); PROTEIN 27.4g; CARBOHYDRATES 6.2g; FIBER 0.6g; CHOLESTEROL 71mg; IRON 0.7mg; SODIUM 297mg; CALCIUM 83mg

Roasted Green Beans with Prosciutto

prep: 4 minutes • **cook:** 16 minutes

POINTS value: 1

- 1 (12-ounce) package pretrimmed green beans
- 1 medium Vidalia or other sweet onion
- 2 ounces prosciutto, thinly sliced
- 2 teaspoons olive oil
- ⅛ teaspoon freshly ground black pepper

1. Preheat oven to 450°.
2. Place first 3 ingredients on a jelly-roll pan; drizzle with olive oil. Sprinkle with pepper, tossing to coat.
3. Spread bean mixture in a single layer on pan. Bake at 450° for 16 minutes, stirring after 10 minutes. Serve immediately. **Yield:** 4 servings (serving size: ¾ cup).

Per serving: CALORIES 87 (39% from fat); FAT 3.8g (saturated fat 0.8g); PROTEIN 5.5g; CARBOHYDRATES 9.4g; FIBER 3.5g; CHOLESTEROL 11mg; IRON 0.7mg; SODIUM 384mg; CALCIUM 51mg

Pork Chops with Tarragon-Onion Gravy

prep: 2 minutes • **cook:** 14 minutes   *POINTS* value: 6

When your family tastes these tender pork chops smothered in a homestyle gravy, they'll never suspect you made dinner at the last minute. Because the chops are very thin, they cook quickly so be careful not to overcook them, which will make them tough.

8	(2-ounce) boneless center-cut loin pork chops (¼ inch thick)
½	teaspoon salt
¼	teaspoon black pepper
¼	cup all-purpose flour
1	tablespoon olive oil
½	cup thinly sliced onion
¾	cup fat-free, less-sodium beef broth
1	tablespoon chopped fresh tarragon

1. Sprinkle pork chops evenly with salt and pepper. Dredge pork in flour. Heat oil in a large skillet over medium-high heat. Add half of pork to pan; cook 1 to 2 minutes on each side or until pork is browned. Transfer pork to a plate. Repeat procedure with remaining pork. Reduce heat to medium. Add onion to pan, and cook 3 minutes or until tender.

2. Stir in beef broth, scraping pan to loosen browned bits. Return pork and any accumulated juices to pan. Bring to a boil; reduce heat, cover, and cook 4 minutes or until pork is done. Stir in tarragon. **Yield:** 4 servings (serving size: 2 pork chops and ½ cup gravy).

Per serving: CALORIES 259 (50% from fat); FAT 14.4g (saturated fat 4.6g); PROTEIN 22.7g; CARBOHYDRATES 9g; FIBER 0.6g; CHOLESTEROL 59mg; IRON 1.1mg; SODIUM 803mg; CALCIUM 25mg

---

Menu
POINTS value
per serving: 8

Pork Chops with Tarragon-Onion Gravy

½ cup microwavable mashed potatoes
POINTS value: 2

Game Plan
1. Cook pork chops.

2. While broth mixture cooks:
• Microwave potatoes.

Menu
POINTS value
per serving: 8

Sweet-Spiced Grilled Lamb Chops

Bulgur-Golden Raisin Pilaf

Game Plan

1. While grill heats:
  • Prepare pilaf.
  • Prepare rub; season lamb.

2. While pilaf stands:
  • Cook lamb.

Sweet-Spiced Grilled Lamb Chops

prep: 2 minutes • **cook:** 8 minutes   **POINTS** value: 5

On cold days when you don't want to brave the outdoor grill, broil these lamb chops in the oven instead.

¾ teaspoon ground cinnamon
½ teaspoon freshly ground black pepper
¼ teaspoon ground allspice
¼ teaspoon ground cumin
⅛ teaspoon salt
⅛ teaspoon ground red pepper
8 (4-ounce) lamb loin chops, trimmed (about 1 inch thick)
Cooking spray
Lime wedges (optional)

1. Prepare grill.
2. Combine first 6 ingredients in a small bowl. Rub mixture evenly over lamb. Place lamb on grill rack coated with cooking spray. Grill 4 to 5 minutes on each side or until desired degree of doneness. Serve with lime wedges, if desired. **Yield:** 4 servings (serving size: 2 lamb chops).

Per serving: CALORIES 209 (40% from fat); FAT 9g (saturated fat 3.3g); PROTEIN 28.7g; CARBOHYDRATES 0.7g; FIBER 0.4g; CHOLESTEROL 90mg; IRON 2.1mg; SODIUM 153mg; CALCIUM 26mg

Bulgur–Golden Raisin Pilaf

prep: 3 minutes • **cook:** 11 minutes • **other:** 2 minutes   **POINTS** value: 3

1 cup water
½ cup bulgur wheat with soy grits hot cereal (such as Hodgson Mill)
½ cup golden raisins
¼ teaspoon crushed red pepper
¼ cup slivered almonds, toasted
2 teaspoons butter
¼ teaspoon salt

1. Combine first 4 ingredients in a medium saucepan; bring to a boil. Cover, reduce heat, and simmer 8 minutes or until water is almost absorbed.
2. Remove from heat; stir in remaining ingredients. Let stand, uncovered, 2 minutes. **Yield:** 4 servings (serving size: ½ cup).

Per serving: CALORIES 176 (31% from fat); FAT 6g (saturated fat 1.5g); PROTEIN 7.2g; CARBOHYDRATES 28.8g; FIBER 3.2g; CHOLESTEROL 5mg; IRON 1.6mg; SODIUM 161mg; CALCIUM 49mg

Poultry

POINTS value: 0
Grilled Squash, Red Bell Pepper, and Onion | page 103
Fast Asian Slaw | page 107

POINTS value: 1
Sweet Lemon-Mint Pear Salad | page 94
Creamy Honey Mustard Slaw | page 95
Honey-Spiced Pineapple | page 97
Garlic Broccolini | page 100
Pan-Roasted Tomatoes with Herbs | page 102
Warm Balsamic Potato Salad | page 108
Heirloom Tomato Salad | page 110
Sautéed Garlicky Spinach | page 111
Roasted Brussels Sprouts à l'Orange | page 112

POINTS value: 2
Sesame Wonton Crisps | page 92
Cumin Corn | page 93
Kalamata Barley | page 99
Grilled Corn on the Cob with Chive Butter | page 101

POINTS value: 3
Almond-Coconut Rice | page 96

POINTS value: 4
Cumin-Seared Chicken with
    Pineapple-Mint Salsa | page 96

POINTS value: 5
Chicken-Veggie Noodle Bowl | page 92
Mexican-Style Lettuce Wraps | page 93
Apricot-Lemon Chicken | page 94

POINTS value: 6
Tomato, Chicken, and Feta Pasta | page 91
Barbecue Chicken with Grilled Peaches | page 95
Tarragon Chicken | page 99
Grilled Chicken with Rustic Mustard Cream | page 102
Grilled Chicken with Herb Sauce | page 103
Chicken and Edamame Stir-Fry | page 104
Turkey Cutlets with Cranberry-Cherry Sauce | page 112

POINTS value: 7
Chili-and-Basil Chicken Noodle Stir-Fry | page 97
Herb-Crusted Chicken with Feta Sauce | page 98
Chicken Scallopine with Pesto and Cheese | page 100
Grilled Chicken Breasts with Queso Verde
    Sauce | page 101
Sweet Mustard Chicken Thighs | page 108
Spicy Chicken Fajitas | page 109
Crunchy Oven-Fried Chicken | page 110
Turkey Cutlets with Balsamic–Brown Sugar
    Sauce | page 111

POINTS value: 8
Chicken-Tortilla Pie | page 90
Chicken Mozzarella and Penne | page 105
Chicken with Asian Peanut Sauce | page 106
Hoisin-Glazed Chicken Thighs | page 107

Menu
POINTS value
per serving: 8

Chicken-Tortilla Pie

Game Plan

1. Prepare chicken mixture.

2. Assemble pie.

3. Bake pie.

Chicken-Tortilla Pie

prep: 13 minutes • **cook:** 10 minutes   *POINTS* value: 8

The fresh salsa called for here has a natural low-sodium advantage over bottled commercial salsa. Look for it in the produce section of your supermarket.

  2 cups shredded cooked chicken breast
  ¼ cup fresh salsa
  1 cup spicy black bean dip (such as Guiltless Gourmet)
  4 (8-inch) multigrain flour tortillas (such as Tumaro's)
  ½ cup (2 ounces) reduced-fat shredded Monterey Jack cheese
Cooking spray

1. Preheat oven to 450°.
2. Combine chicken and salsa in a medium bowl.
3. Spread ¼ cup black bean dip over each tortilla. Top each evenly with chicken mixture and 2 tablespoons cheese. Stack tortillas in bottom of a 9-inch springform pan coated with cooking spray. Bake at 450° for 10 minutes or until thoroughly heated and cheese melts. Remove sides of pan. Cut pie into 4 wedges. Serve immediately. **Yield:** 4 servings (serving size: 1 wedge).

Per serving: CALORIES 380 (26% from fat); FAT 11g (saturated fat 4.3g); PROTEIN 39.9g; CARBOHYDRATES 28.7g; FIBER 12.2g; CHOLESTEROL 80mg; IRON 0.8mg; SODIUM 660mg; CALCIUM 215mg

Tomato, Chicken, and Feta Pasta

prep: 1 minute • **cook:** 14 minutes

POINTS value: 6

This easy-to-prepare pasta dish is delicious served warm or chilled. Store any leftovers for tomorrow's lunch. To save time, start heating the water for the pasta first, and then prepare the other ingredients while the water comes to a boil.

  4 ounces uncooked penne (about 1 cup)
  1 teaspoon olive oil
  1 teaspoon minced garlic
  1 (14.5-ounce) can diced tomatoes with basil, garlic, and oregano, undrained
  3 cups chopped cooked chicken breast
  ¼ cup sliced pitted kalamata olives
  ¼ teaspoon freshly ground black pepper
  6 tablespoons crumbled feta cheese with basil and sun-dried tomatoes

1. Cook pasta according to package directions, omitting salt and fat.

2. While pasta cooks, heat oil in a medium nonstick skillet over medium heat. Add garlic, and cook 30 seconds. Add tomatoes and next 3 ingredients; simmer 6 minutes or until thoroughly heated, stirring occasionally.

3. When pasta is done, drain and return to pan. Add tomato mixture to pasta; toss gently, and top with feta cheese. Serve immediately. **Yield:** 6 servings (serving size: about 1 cup).

Per serving: CALORIES 259 (24% from fat); FAT 6.9g (saturated fat 2g); PROTEIN 27g; CARBOHYDRATES 20.8g; FIBER 1.1g; CHOLESTEROL 66mg; IRON 2mg; SODIUM 597mg; CALCIUM 82mg

---

Menu
POINTS value per serving: 6

Tomato, Chicken, and Feta Pasta

1 cup arugula salad with grape tomatoes and fat-free balsamic vinaigrette
POINTS value: 0

Game Plan

1. While water for pasta comes to a boil:
  • Mince garlic.

2. While pasta cooks:
  • Prepare sauce.

3. Toss pasta.

4. Assemble salad.

pictured on page 47

Chicken-Veggie Noodle Bowl

prep: 6 minutes • **cook:** 13 minutes

POINTS value: 5

You can usually buy dried Thai chiles in the international aisle of the grocery store, while fresh ones are available at Asian markets. If you can't find either of them, use Fresno, serrano, or other small hot red chiles.

8 ounces uncooked whole-grain spaghetti (such as Barilla)
2 cups shredded skinless, boneless rotisserie chicken breast
3 cups shredded napa (Chinese) cabbage
1 cup matchstick-cut carrots
1 cup thinly sliced green onions
1 red bell pepper, julienne-cut into 2-inch strips
½ cup low-fat sesame ginger dressing (such as Newman's Own)
1 red Thai chile, seeded and thinly sliced (optional)
¼ cup chopped fresh mint
2 tablespoons chopped unsalted, dry-roasted peanuts

1. Cook spaghetti according to package directions, omitting salt and fat. Drain and rinse with cold water; drain.
2. Combine spaghetti, chicken, cabbage, and next 4 ingredients in a large bowl; add chile, if desired, and toss well. Spoon evenly onto plates; sprinkle evenly with mint and peanuts. **Yield:** 6 servings (serving size: about 1¾ cups pasta mixture, 2 teaspoons mint, and 1 teaspoon peanuts).

Per serving: CALORIES 286 (18% from fat); FAT 5.8g (saturated fat 0.8g); PROTEIN 20.8g; CARBOHYDRATES 37.8g; FIBER 6.5g; CHOLESTEROL 40mg; IRON 2.2mg; SODIUM 465mg; CALCIUM 63mg

Sesame Wonton Crisps

prep: 5 minutes • **cook:** 5 minutes

POINTS value: 2

2 teaspoons dark sesame oil
1 teaspoon water
18 wonton wrappers
Cooking spray
1 teaspoon sesame seeds
¼ teaspoon salt
⅛ teaspoon five-spice powder

1. Preheat oven to 400°.
2. Combine sesame oil and 1 teaspoon water in a small bowl. Set aside.
3. Place wonton wrappers on a baking sheet coated with cooking spray. Brush evenly with oil mixture. Sprinkle evenly with sesame seeds, salt, and five-spice powder.
4. Bake at 400° for 5 minutes or until browned and crispy. **Yield:** 6 servings (serving size: 3 wonton crisps).

Per serving: CALORIES 88 (25% from fat); FAT 2g (saturated fat 0.3g); PROTEIN 2.6g; CARBOHYDRATES 14.2g; FIBER 0.5g; CHOLESTEROL 2mg; IRON 0.9mg; SODIUM 234mg; CALCIUM 17mg

Mexican-Style Lettuce Wraps

prep: 7 minutes   **POINTS** value: 5

Chopped cooked chicken, salsa, cheese, and olives are nestled in tender Bibb lettuce leaves. For a crunchier variation, try crisp iceberg lettuce leaves.

   1   cup chopped cooked chicken breast
   ½   cup chopped grape tomatoes
   ¼   cup (1 ounce) preshredded reduced-fat sharp Cheddar cheese
   ¼   cup sliced ripe olives
   6   tablespoons chipotle salsa
   2   tablespoons chopped fresh cilantro
Light sour cream (optional)
   6   Bibb lettuce leaves
   2   lime wedges

1. Combine first 4 ingredients in a medium bowl; toss well. Layer ⅓ cup chicken mixture, 1 tablespoon salsa, 1 teaspoon cilantro, and sour cream, if desired, on each lettuce leaf. Fold in edges of leaves; roll up, and secure each wrap with wooden picks. Serve with lime wedges. **Yield:** 2 servings (serving size: 3 wraps).

Per serving: CALORIES 228 (47% from fat); FAT 12g (saturated fat 4.5g); PROTEIN 23g; CARBOHYDRATES 7.9g; FIBER 2.5g; CHOLESTEROL 67mg; IRON 1.8mg; SODIUM 698mg; CALCIUM 255mg

Menu
POINTS value
per serving: 7

Mexican-Style Lettuce Wraps
Cumin Corn

Game Plan

1. Prepare and measure ingredients for wraps.

2. Remove corn from cob.

3. While corn mixture cooks:
   • Assemble wraps.

Cumin Corn

prep: 3 minutes • **cook:** 10 minutes   **POINTS** value: 2

   2   ears corn
   2   teaspoons butter
   ¼   cup refrigerated prechopped onion
   ¼   cup refrigerated prechopped tricolor bell pepper
   ¼   teaspoon ground cumin
   ⅛   teaspoon salt
   ⅛   teaspoon black pepper

1. Remove husks from corn; scrub silks from corn. Cut kernels from ears of corn; set corn aside. Discard cobs.
2. Melt butter in a nonstick skillet over medium heat. Add onion and bell pepper; cook, stirring constantly, 3 to 4 minutes or until crisp-tender. Stir in cumin, salt, and black pepper; cook 1 minute. Stir in corn; cook 5 minutes or until corn is crisp-tender, stirring frequently. **Yield:** 2 servings (serving size: ½ cup).

Per serving: CALORIES 122 (37% from fat); FAT 5g (saturated fat 2.6g); PROTEIN 3.3g; CARBOHYDRATES 19.6g; FIBER 3.1g; CHOLESTEROL 10mg; IRON 0.7mg; SODIUM 187mg; CALCIUM 10mg

Menu
POINTS value
per serving: 6

Apricot-Lemon Chicken

Sweet Lemon-Mint Pear Salad

Game Plan

1. Zest and juice lemons.

2. While chicken cooks:
• Prepare salad.

Apricot-Lemon Chicken

prep: 4 minutes • **cook:** 14 minutes   **POINTS** value: 5

Start with an apricot fruit spread for a sauce that transforms simply prepared chicken breasts into this elegant dish.

    1   teaspoon curry powder
    ½   teaspoon salt
    ¼   teaspoon freshly ground black pepper
    4   (6-ounce) skinless, boneless chicken breast halves
    Cooking spray
    ⅓   cup apricot spread (such as Polaner All Fruit)
    2   tablespoons fresh lemon juice
    2   tablespoons water
    2   teaspoons grated fresh lemon rind

1. Combine first 3 ingredients in a small bowl; rub mixture over chicken.
2. Place a large nonstick skillet over medium-high heat. Coat pan with cooking spray. Cook chicken 6 minutes on each side or until done. Remove chicken from pan, and keep warm.
3. Add apricot spread, lemon juice, and 2 tablespoons water to pan, stirring until smooth. Cook over medium heat 1 minute. Spoon sauce over chicken; sprinkle with lemon rind. **Yield:** 4 servings (serving size: 1 chicken breast half and about 1½ tablespoons apricot-lemon sauce).

Per serving: CALORIES 245 (8% from fat); FAT 2g (saturated fat 0.6g); PROTEIN 39.4g; CARBOHYDRATES 14.5g; FIBER 0.3g; CHOLESTEROL 99mg; IRON 1.4mg; SODIUM 402mg; CALCIUM 24mg

Sweet Lemon-Mint Pear Salad

prep: 7 minutes   **POINTS** value: 1

    1   tablespoon sugar
    3   tablespoons fresh lemon juice
    2   teaspoons canola oil
    4   cups packed baby spinach and spring greens mix
    1   firm pear, thinly sliced
    ½   cup sliced red onion
    ¼   cup torn fresh mint leaves

1. Combine first 3 ingredients in a large bowl, stirring with a whisk. Add greens mix and remaining ingredients; toss well. Serve immediately. **Yield:** 4 servings (serving size: 1½ cups).

Per serving: CALORIES 72 (30% from fat); FAT 2g (saturated fat 0.2g); PROTEIN 1g; CARBOHYDRATES 13g; FIBER 2.3g; CHOLESTEROL 0mg; IRON 1mg; SODIUM 20mg; CALCIUM 35mg

Barbecue Chicken with Grilled Peaches

prep: 3 minutes • **cook:** 14 minutes   *POINTS* value: 6

Pairing peaches with barbecue-seasoned chicken is the ultimate summer combination. Grilling caramelizes the sugars in the fruit, enhancing its natural sweetness.

     4   (6-ounce) skinless, boneless chicken breast halves
     2   teaspoons salt-free barbecue seasoning (such as Mrs. Dash Chicken Grilling Blend)
     ¼   teaspoon salt, divided
     ½   cup low-sugar apricot spread (such as Smucker's)
     2   tablespoons white wine vinegar
     1   tablespoon grated peeled fresh ginger
Cooking spray
     4   large ripe peaches, halved and pitted

1. Prepare grill.
2. Sprinkle chicken with barbecue seasoning and ⅛ teaspoon salt.
3. Combine apricot spread, vinegar, ginger, and remaining ⅛ teaspoon salt in a small bowl.
4. Place chicken on grill rack coated with cooking spray; grill 7 minutes on each side or until done, basting occasionally with glaze. Place peach halves on grill rack, cut sides down. Grill 3 minutes on each side or until peaches are soft, basting occasionally with glaze. **Yield:** 4 servings (serving size: 1 chicken breast half and 2 peach halves).

Per serving: CALORIES 300 (8% from fat); FAT 2.5g (saturated fat 0.6g); PROTEIN 40.7g; CARBOHYDRATES 27.2g; FIBER 2.4g; CHOLESTEROL 99mg; IRON 1.6mg; SODIUM 256mg; CALCIUM 28mg

Creamy Honey Mustard Slaw

prep: 4 minutes • **other:** 5 minutes   *POINTS* value: 1

     2   tablespoons light mayonnaise
     1   tablespoon honey Dijon mustard
     2   teaspoons fresh lemon juice
     2   teaspoons sugar
     3   cups cabbage-and-carrot coleslaw

1. Combine first 4 ingredients in a medium bowl, stirring with a whisk. Add coleslaw; toss to combine. **Yield:** 4 servings (serving size: ½ cup).

Per serving: CALORIES 52 (48% from fat); FAT 2.8g (saturated fat 0.5g); PROTEIN 0.6g; CARBOHYDRATES 6.5g; FIBER 0.9g; CHOLESTEROL 3mg; IRON 0.2mg; SODIUM 98mg; CALCIUM 17mg

---

Menu
***POINTS* value**
per serving: 7

Barbecue Chicken with Grilled Peaches

Creamy Honey Mustard Slaw

Game Plan

1. While grill heats:
• Season chicken breasts and prepare glaze.

2. While chicken cooks:
• Prepare slaw.

Cumin-Seared Chicken with Pineapple-Mint Salsa

prep: 1 minute • **cook:** 14 minutes   *POINTS* value: 4

For a tasty variation, try serving this colorful salsa over grilled fish.

    1   teaspoon ground cumin
    ½   teaspoon salt
    ⅛   teaspoon ground red pepper
    4   (6-ounce) skinless, boneless chicken breast halves
        Cooking spray
    1½ cups cubed pineapple, finely chopped
    ½   cup chopped fresh mint
    ¼   cup finely chopped red onion
    2   tablespoons rice vinegar
    2   teaspoons grated peeled fresh ginger

1. Combine cumin, salt, and red pepper; sprinkle evenly over chicken.
2. Heat a large nonstick skillet over medium-high heat. Coat pan with cooking spray. Add chicken; cook 7 to 8 minutes on each side or until done.
3. While chicken cooks, combine pineapple and next 4 ingredients; toss gently to blend. Serve with chicken. **Yield:** 4 servings (serving size: 1 chicken breast half and ½ cup salsa).

Per serving: CALORIES 224 (10% from fat); FAT 2g (saturated fat 0.6g); PROTEIN 39.9g; CARBOHYDRATES 9.2g; FIBER 1.5g; CHOLESTEROL 99mg; IRON 1.8mg; SODIUM 405mg; CALCIUM 41mg

Almond-Coconut Rice

prep: 2 minutes • **cook:** 6 minutes   *POINTS* value: 3

    1   (10-ounce) package frozen whole-grain brown rice
    ⅓   cup slivered almonds
    3   tablespoons flaked sweetened coconut
    ½   teaspoon ground cumin
    ⅛   teaspoon salt

1. Microwave rice according to package directions.
2. While rice cooks, heat a medium nonstick skillet over medium-high heat. Add almonds and coconut; cook 2 minutes or until lightly browned, stirring constantly. Remove from heat; add rice, cumin, and salt, stirring to blend. **Yield:** 4 servings (serving size: ¾ cup).

Per serving: CALORIES 147 (36% from fat); FAT 6g (saturated fat 1.4g); PROTEIN 4.2g; CARBOHYDRATES 19.8g; FIBER 2.5g; CHOLESTEROL 0mg; IRON 0.5mg; SODIUM 86mg; CALCIUM 35mg

Chili-and-Basil Chicken Noodle Stir-Fry

prep: 7 minutes • **cook:** 13 minutes   *POINTS* value: 7

Green onions and basil add a splash of color to this spicy recipe. Sprinkle them over the finished dish just before serving.

Menu
***POINTS* value per serving: 8**

Chili-and-Basil Chicken Noodle Stir-Fry

Honey-Spiced Pineapple

Game Plan

1. While water for pasta comes to a boil:
   • Chop green onions.

2. While pasta cooks:
   • Prepare chicken mixture.

3. Prepare pineapple.

1	(6-ounce) package Japanese noodles (such as Chuka Soba), uncooked and crumbled
3	tablespoons less-sodium soy sauce
2	tablespoons fresh lime juice
1	tablespoon chili garlic sauce
2	teaspoons fish sauce
1	pound skinless, boneless chicken breasts, thinly sliced
¼	cup fat-free, less-sodium chicken broth
1	teaspoon cornstarch
1	tablespoon canola oil
3	green onions, diagonally cut
⅓	cup fresh small basil leaves

1. Cook noodles according to package directions, omitting salt and fat. Drain and keep warm.

2. While pasta cooks, combine soy sauce and next 3 ingredients. Combine chicken and 2 tablespoons soy sauce mixture. Add chicken broth and cornstarch to remaining soy sauce mixture; set aside.

3. Heat oil in a large nonstick skillet over medium-high heat. Add chicken mixture; cook 5 minutes or until done, stirring occasionally. Add noodles and soy sauce mixture; cook 1 minute or until sauce thickens. Top with green onions and basil. Serve immediately. **Yield:** 4 servings (serving size: about 1 cup).

Per serving: CALORIES 327 (16% from fat); FAT 5.7g (saturated fat 0.6g); PROTEIN 32.8g; CARBOHYDRATES 35.4g; FIBER 0.6g; CHOLESTEROL 66mg; IRON 1.4mg; SODIUM 866mg; CALCIUM 27mg

Honey-Spiced Pineapple

prep: 1 minute • **cook:** 4 minutes   *POINTS* value: 1

2	teaspoons butter
2	cups fresh pineapple chunks
1	tablespoon honey
¼	teaspoon curry powder

1. Melt butter in a large nonstick skillet over medium-high heat. Add pineapple, honey, and curry powder; cook 3 minutes or until thoroughly heated, stirring frequently. **Yield:** 4 servings (serving size: ½ cup).

Per serving: CALORIES 71 (25% from fat); FAT 2g (saturated fat 1.2g); PROTEIN 0.5g; CARBOHYDRATES 14.3g; FIBER 1.2g; CHOLESTEROL 5mg; IRON 0.3mg; SODIUM 15mg; CALCIUM 12mg

Menu
POINTS value
per serving: 7

**Herb-Crusted Chicken
with Feta Sauce**

1 cup roasted zucchini strips
POINTS value: 0

Game Plan

1. While oven preheats:
• Cut zucchini and assemble
on pan.
• Prepare feta sauce.

2. While zucchini cooks:
• Prepare chicken.

Herb-Crusted Chicken with Feta Sauce

prep: 6 minutes • **cook:** 11 minutes

POINTS value: 7

A tangy Greek sauce made of mint, lemon, and feta cheese is a welcome addition to succulent breaded chicken breast. Use leftover sauce as a dressing spooned over romaine lettuce or tossed with fresh veggies such as tomatoes and cucumbers. A 1½-tablespoon serving has a *POINTS* value of 1.

1   lemon
1   tablespoon chopped fresh mint
4   teaspoons extra-virgin olive oil
Dash of black pepper
1   (3.5-ounce) package reduced-fat feta cheese
⅔   cup whole wheat panko (Japanese breadcrumbs)
2   tablespoons Italian seasoning
4   (6-ounce) skinless, boneless chicken breast halves
½   teaspoon salt
¼   teaspoon black pepper
4   teaspoons olive oil

1. Grate rind and squeeze juice from lemon to measure ½ teaspoon rind and 2 tablespoons juice. Combine rind, juice, mint, 4 teaspoons oil, and pepper in a small bowl, stirring with a whisk. Add cheese; toss gently. Reserve 6 tablespoons of sauce to serve with cooked chicken. Cover and chill remaining sauce for another use.
2. Combine panko and Italian seasoning in a shallow bowl. Sprinkle chicken with salt and pepper; dredge in panko mixture.
3. Heat 4 teaspoons oil in a large nonstick skillet over medium-high heat. Add chicken; cook 5 minutes or until browned. Turn chicken over; reduce heat to medium, and cook 5 minutes or until done. Place 1 chicken breast half on each of 4 plates, and spoon 1½ tablespoons feta sauce over each serving. **Yield:** 4 servings (serving size: 1 chicken breast half and 1½ tablespoons sauce).

Per serving: CALORIES 323 (37% from fat); FAT 13.3g (saturated fat 3.4g); PROTEIN 39.3g; CARBOHYDRATES 10.3g; FIBER 1.6g; CHOLESTEROL 98mg; IRON 1.8mg; SODIUM 584mg; CALCIUM 51mg

Tarragon Chicken

prep: 4 minutes • **cook:** 7 minutes

POINTS value: 6

Add the remaining olive oil–tarragon mixture at the final stage of the cooking process to preserve its full-bodied taste and citrus essence.

- 4 (6-ounce) skinless, boneless chicken breast halves
- ¼ teaspoon salt
- 2 tablespoons extra-virgin olive oil
- 1 teaspoon grated fresh lemon rind
- 2 tablespoons fresh lemon juice
- 1 garlic clove, minced
- 2 teaspoons minced fresh tarragon
- ⅛ teaspoon salt

1. Place each chicken breast half between 2 sheets of heavy-duty plastic wrap; pound to ¼-inch thickness using a meat mallet or small heavy skillet. Sprinkle chicken evenly with ¼ teaspoon salt.
2. Combine olive oil and next 5 ingredients in a small bowl, stirring well with a whisk. Heat a large nonstick skillet over medium-high heat. Add 2 teaspoons oil mixture to pan, spreading evenly over bottom of pan with a wide spatula. Add chicken; cook 2 minutes. Drizzle chicken with 2 teaspoons oil mixture. Turn chicken breasts over; cook 2 minutes. Drizzle remaining oil mixture over chicken; reduce heat to low. Cover and cook 2 minutes or until done. Transfer chicken to a serving platter. Pour pan drippings over chicken; serve immediately. **Yield:** 4 servings (serving size: 1 chicken breast half).

Per calories: CALORIES 251 (33% from fat); FAT 9g (saturated fat 1.6g); PROTEIN 39.4g; CARBOHYDRATES 1.1g; FIBER 0.1g; CHOLESTEROL 99mg; IRON 1.3mg; SODIUM 329mg; CALCIUM 23mg

Kalamata Barley

prep: 1 minute • **cook:** 13 minutes • **other:** 5 minutes

POINTS value: 2

- 1⅓ cups water
- ⅔ cup uncooked quick-cooking barley (such as Quaker)
- ½ cup refrigerated prechopped tricolor bell pepper
- 10 pitted kalamata olives, chopped
- 2 tablespoons chopped fresh parsley
- 1 teaspoon extra-virgin olive oil
- ⅛ teaspoon salt

1. Bring 1⅓ cups water to a boil in a medium saucepan; add barley. Cover and cook 12 minutes. Remove pan from heat; stir in bell pepper and remaining ingredients. Let stand 5 minutes; fluff with a fork before serving. **Yield:** 4 servings (serving size: about ½ cup).

Per serving: CALORIES 122 (29% from fat); FAT 4g (saturated fat 0.5g); PROTEIN 2.9g; CARBOHYDRATES 20.5g; FIBER 3g; CHOLESTEROL 0mg; IRON 0.6mg; SODIUM 227mg; CALCIUM 8mg

---

Menu
POINTS value
per serving: 8

Tarragon Chicken

Kalamata Barley

Game Plan

1. While water for barley comes to a boil:
- Measure barley.

2. While barley cooks:
- Prepare chicken.

3. While barley stands:
- Chop parsley and olives.

4. Toss barley.

Menu
POINTS value
per serving: 8

Chicken Scallopine with Pesto and Cheese

Garlic Broccolini

Game Plan

1. Trim broccolini and slice garlic.

2. While broccolini cooks in microwave:
• Pound and season chicken.
• Cook garlic.

3. Sauté broccolini.

4. While broccolini cooks in water:
• Cook chicken.

Chicken Scallopine with Pesto and Cheese

prep: 3 minutes • **cook:** 11 minutes   ***POINTS*** value: 7

  4   (6-ounce) skinless, boneless chicken breast halves
  ¼   teaspoon salt
  ¼   teaspoon freshly ground black pepper
  1   tablespoon olive oil
  ½   cup Marsala wine
  2   tablespoons commercial pesto
  4   (0.7-ounce) slices part-skim mozzarella cheese

1. Place chicken breast halves between 2 sheets of heavy-duty plastic wrap; pound to ¼-inch thickness using a meat mallet or small heavy skillet. Sprinkle chicken with salt and pepper.
2. Heat oil in a large skillet over medium-high heat. Add chicken; cook 3 minutes on each side. Remove chicken from pan; keep warm. Reduce heat to medium-low. Add Marsala to pan, scraping pan to loosen browned bits.
3. Spread 1½ tablespoon pesto over each chicken breast; top each with 1 slice cheese. Return chicken to pan; cover and cook over medium-low heat 4 minutes or until done. **Yield:** 4 servings (serving size: 1 chicken breast half and about 1 tablespoon sauce).

Per serving: CALORIES 321 (33% from fat); FAT 11.8g (saturated fat 3.2g); PROTEIN 43.7g; CARBOHYDRATES 3.5g; FIBER 0g; CHOLESTEROL 108mg; IRON 1.3mg; SODIUM 349mg; CALCIUM 145mg

Garlic Broccolini

prep: 2 minutes • **cook:** 18 minutes   ***POINTS*** value: 1

  1   pound broccolini, trimmed
  1   tablespoon olive oil
  4   garlic cloves, sliced
  3   tablespoons water
  1   tablespoon fresh lemon juice
  ¼   teaspoon salt

1. Place broccolini in a large microwave-safe bowl. Cover and microwave at HIGH 4 minutes or until crisp-tender.
2. While broccolini cooks, heat oil in a large nonstick skillet over medium heat. Add garlic; sauté 1 minute or until golden. Remove garlic from pan. Add broccolini; sauté 2 minutes. Add 3 tablespoons water; cover and cook 12 minutes or until tender. Stir in reserved garlic and remaining ingredients. **Yield:** 4 servings (serving size: about ½ cup).

Per serving: CALORIES 67 (52% from fat); FAT 3.9g (saturated fat 0.6g); PROTEIN 3.6g; CARBOHYDRATES 7.2g; FIBER 3.5g; CHOLESTEROL 0mg; IRON 1mg; SODIUM 177mg; CALCIUM 6mg

Grilled Chicken Breasts with Queso Verde Sauce

prep: 2 minutes • **cook:** 15 minutes   *POINTS* value: 7

Two simple ingredients combine to yield a restaurant-quality cheese sauce, taking simple grilled chicken to another level.

  4   (6-ounce) skinless, boneless chicken breast halves
  2   teaspoons olive oil
  2   teaspoons salt-free Fiesta lime seasoning (such as Mrs. Dash)
Cooking spray
  6   (0.7-ounce) slices white American cheese, torn
  ⅓   cup salsa verde (such as Herdez)
Chopped tomato (optional)
Chopped fresh cilantro (optional)

1. Prepare grill.
2. Brush chicken breast halves with oil; sprinkle evenly with seasoning. Place chicken on grill rack coated with cooking spray; grill 6 minutes on each side or until chicken is done.
3. Place cheese and salsa verde in a microwave-safe bowl. Microwave at HIGH 2 minutes or until cheese melts and mixture is smooth, stirring every 30 seconds. Spoon cheese sauce over chicken; sprinkle with chopped tomato and cilantro, if desired. Serve immediately. **Yield:** 4 servings (serving size: 1 chicken breast half and about 2½ tablespoons cheese sauce).

Per serving: CALORIES 317 (38% from fat); FAT 13.4g (saturated fat 8.6g); PROTEIN 45.7g; CARBOHYDRATES 1.3g; FIBER 0g; CHOLESTEROL 118mg; IRON 1.2mg; SODIUM 534mg; CALORIES 212mg

Grilled Corn on the Cob with Chive Butter

prep: 3 minutes • **cook:** 12 minutes   *POINTS* value: 2

  4   ears shucked corn
Cooking spray
  2   tablespoons light stick butter, softened
  1   tablespoon chopped fresh chives

1. Prepare grill.
2. Coat corn with cooking spray. Place corn on grill rack; cover and grill 6 minutes on each side or until slightly charred.
3. While corn grills, combine butter and chives. Brush butter mixture over grilled corn. **Yield:** 4 servings (serving size: 1 ear of corn).

Per serving: CALORIES 103 (36% from fat); FAT 4.1g (saturated fat 1.9g); PROTEIN 2.9g; CARBOHYDRATES 17.7g; FIBER 2.5g; CHOLESTEROL 8mg; IRON 0.5mg; SODIUM 61mg; CALCIUM 2mg

Menu
***POINTS* value**
per serving: 9

Grilled Chicken Breasts with Queso Verde Sauce

Grilled Corn on the Cob with Chive Butter

Game Plan

1. While grill heats:
• Remove husks from corn; chop chives.
• Season chicken.

2. Cook chicken and corn.

3. While chicken and corn cook:
• Prepare chive butter.
• Prepare queso verde sauce.

Grilled Chicken with Rustic Mustard Cream

prep: 6 minutes • **cook:** 12 minutes

POINTS value: 6

Menu
POINTS value
per serving: 7

Grilled Chicken with Rustic Mustard Cream

Pan-Roasted Tomatoes with Herbs

Game Plan

1. While grill heats:
- Chop oregano and rosemary.
- Prepare chicken for grill.

2. While chicken cooks:
- Prepare mustard cream.
- Prepare tomatoes.

A flavorful combination of rosemary, olive oil, and Dijon mustard gives this chicken a Mediterranean flair.

 1   tablespoon plus 1 teaspoon whole-grain Dijon mustard, divided
 1   tablespoon olive oil
 1   teaspoon chopped fresh rosemary
 ¼   teaspoon salt
 ¼   teaspoon black pepper
 4   (6-ounce) skinless, boneless chicken breast halves
Cooking spray
 3   tablespoons light mayonnaise
 1   tablespoon water
Rosemary sprigs (optional)

1. Prepare grill.
2. Combine 1 teaspoon mustard, oil, and next 3 ingredients in a small bowl; brush evenly over chicken. Place chicken on grill rack coated with cooking spray; grill 6 minutes on each side or until done.
3. While chicken grills, combine remaining 1 tablespoon mustard, mayonnaise, and 1 tablespoon water in a bowl; stir with a whisk. Serve mustard cream with grilled chicken. Garnish with rosemary sprigs, if desired. **Yield:** 4 servings (serving size: 1 chicken breast half and 1 tablespoon mustard cream).

Per serving: CALORIES 262 (34% from fat); FAT 10g (saturated fat 1.8g); PROTEIN 39.6g; CARBOHYDRATES 1.7g; FIBER 0.2g; CHOLESTEROL 102mg; IRON 1.4mg; SODIUM 448mg; CALCIUM 25mg

Pan-Roasted Tomatoes with Herbs

prep: 2 minutes • **cook:** 4 minutes • **other:** 5 minutes

POINTS value: 1

 2   teaspoons olive oil, divided
 1   pint multicolored grape tomatoes
 1   teaspoon chopped fresh oregano
 ½   teaspoon chopped fresh rosemary
 ¼   teaspoon salt
 ¼   teaspoon crushed red pepper

1. Heat 1 teaspoon oil in a medium nonstick skillet over medium-high heat. Add tomatoes; cook 3 to 4 minutes or until tomatoes begin to blister. Remove from heat; stir in remaining 1 teaspoon oil and remaining ingredients, tossing gently to combine. Let stand 5 minutes. **Yield:** 4 servings (serving size: ½ cup).

Per serving: CALORIES 34 (66% from fat); FAT 3g (saturated fat 0.4g); PROTEIN 0.7g; CARBOHYDRATES 3.1g; FIBER 0.9g; CHOLESTEROL 0mg; IRON 0.2mg; SODIUM 149mg; CALCIUM 10mg

Grilled Chicken with Herb Sauce

prep: 6 minutes • **cook:** 10 minutes

POINTS value: 6

   4   (6-ounce) skinless, boneless chicken breast halves
   ¾   teaspoon kosher salt, divided
   ½   teaspoon freshly ground black pepper
   Cooking spray
   2   tablespoons fresh oregano leaves
   2   tablespoons fresh Italian parsley leaves
   2   garlic cloves
   2   medium shallots, peeled and quartered
   3   tablespoons white wine vinegar
   3   tablespoons water
   2   tablespoons extra-virgin olive oil
   ½   teaspoon crushed red pepper flakes

1. Prepare grill.
2. Sprinkle chicken with ¼ teaspoon salt and pepper; coat with cooking spray.
Place chicken on grill rack coated with cooking spray, and grill 5 minutes on each
side or until done.
3. Combine remaining ½ teaspoon salt, oregano, and next 7 ingredients in a food
processor. Pulse 8 to 10 times or until finely chopped, stopping to scrape down
sides as needed. Serve herb sauce over chicken. **Yield:** 4 servings (serving size:
1 chicken breast half and 2 tablespoons herb sauce).

Per serving: CALORIES 264 (32% from fat); FAT 9.3g (saturated fat 1.6g); PROTEIN 39.9g; CARBOHYDRATES 3.6g; FIBER 0.3g; CHOLESTEROL 99mg; IRON 1.6mg;
SODIUM 474mg; CALCIUM 40mg

Grilled Squash, Red Bell Pepper, and Onion

prep: 3 minutes • **cook:** 6 minutes

POINTS value: 0

   2   yellow squash, cut into ¼-inch slices
   1   red bell pepper, halved and seeded
   1   red onion, cut into ¼-inch slices
   Cooking spray
   ¼   teaspoon salt
   ¼   teaspoon black pepper

1. Prepare grill.
2. Coat vegetables with cooking spray; sprinkle with salt and pepper.
3. Place vegetables on grill rack coated with cooking spray. Grill vegetables 3 minutes on each side. Coarsely chop vegetables. **Yield:** 4 servings (serving size: about
1 cup vegetables).

Per serving: CALORIES 34 (8% from fat); FAT 0.3g (saturated fat 0.1g); PROTEIN 1.8g; CARBOHYDRATES 7.7g; FIBER 2.2g; CHOLESTEROL 0mg; IRON 0.5mg;
SODIUM 150mg; CALCIUM 23mg

Menu
POINTS value
per serving: 6

**Grilled Chicken with
Herb Sauce**

**Grilled Squash, Red Bell
Pepper, and Onion**

Game Plan

1. While grill heats:
  • Cut squash, red bell pepper,
    and onion.
  • Season vegetables and
    chicken breasts.

2. Grill chicken and vegetables.

3. Prepare herb sauce.

Menu
POINTS value
per serving: 7

Chicken and Edamame Stir-Fry

1 orange
POINTS value: 1

Game Plan

1. Microwave rice.

2. Prepare chicken mixture.

3. Cut orange into wedges.

Chicken and Edamame Stir-Fry

prep: 4 minutes • **cook:** 11 minutes   *POINTS* value: 6

Oyster sauce is a thick, dark brown sauce commonly used in Asian cuisines. You can find it in Asian markets or in the Asian section of your grocery store. Serve with orange wedges for a simple, sweet side dish.

> 1   (8.5-ounce) package precooked jasmine rice (such as Uncle Ben's Ready Rice)
> ¼   cup water
> 2   tablespoons less-sodium soy sauce (such as Kikkoman)
> 2   tablespoons oyster sauce
> 2   teaspoons rice vinegar
> 2   teaspoons canola oil
> 1   pound chicken cutlets (about 6 cutlets), cut into strips
> 1   cup red bell pepper strips
> 1   cup frozen shelled edamame (green soybeans)
> ¼   cup chopped fresh cilantro

1. Microwave rice according to package directions; keep warm.
2. Combine ¼ cup water and next 3 ingredients in a small bowl, stirring with a whisk. Heat oil in a large nonstick skillet over medium-high heat. Add chicken, and cook 6 minutes or until browned, stirring frequently. Add bell pepper and edamame; cook 3 minutes or until vegetables are crisp-tender, stirring frequently. Add soy sauce mixture; cook 1 minute, stirring constantly. Remove from heat, and stir in cilantro. Serve chicken mixture over rice. **Yield:** 4 servings (serving size: 1 cup chicken mixture and about ⅓ cup rice).

Per serving: CALORIES 290 (19% from fat); FAT 6.2g (saturated fat 0.6g); PROTEIN 32g; CARBOHYDRATES 25.3g; FIBER 2.4g; CHOLESTEROL 66mg; IRON 2.3mg; SODIUM 629mg; CALCIUM 43mg

pictured on cover

Chicken Mozzarella and Penne

prep: 5 minutes • **cook:** 15 minutes   **POINTS** value: 8

You can use boneless chicken breast halves for this recipe. Just trim them down to size and pound slightly before cooking. If your basil leaves are large, tear them into small pieces.

- 3 ounces uncooked penne pasta (such as Barilla PLUS)
- 1 cup Italian-seasoned panko (Japanese breadcrumbs)
- ½ cup egg substitute
- 4 (4-ounce) chicken cutlets
- 1 tablespoon olive oil
- ⅛ teaspoon black pepper
- 1 (26-ounce) jar tomato and basil pasta sauce (such as Classico), divided
- ½ cup (2 ounces) shredded part-skim mozzarella cheese
- ¼ cup packed small fresh basil leaves

1. Cook pasta according to package directions, omitting salt and fat; drain. Cover and keep warm.
2. While pasta cooks, place panko in a shallow dish. Place egg substitute in a bowl. Dip chicken in egg substitute; dredge in panko, pressing firmly.
3. Heat oil in a large nonstick skillet over medium-high heat. Add chicken; cook 4 minutes on each side or until done. Remove chicken from pan; sprinkle with pepper. Remove pan from heat. Add pasta sauce to pan, scraping pan to loosen browned bits. Return pan to heat. Cover and cook over medium-high heat 2 minutes or until thoroughly heated.
4. Spoon pasta evenly onto each of 4 serving plates; top each with a chicken cutlet. Spoon sauce evenly over chicken. Sprinkle with cheese and basil leaves.
Yield: 4 servings (serving size: 1 cutlet, about ½ cup sauce, ½ cup pasta, and 1 tablespoon basil leaves).

Per serving: CALORIES 388 (24% from fat); FAT 10.2g (saturated fat 2.4g); PROTEIN 39.1g; CARBOHYDRATES 35g; FIBER 5.5g; CHOLESTEROL 74mg; IRON 8mg; SODIUM 899mg; CALCIUM 236mg

Menu
POINTS value
per serving: 8

Chicken Mozzarella and Penne

Game Plan

1. While water for pasta comes to a boil:
 • Dredge chicken in panko.

2. While pasta cooks:
 • Cook chicken and sauce.

Menu
POINTS value
per serving: 8

**Chicken with Asian
Peanut Sauce**

Game Plan

1. Juice lime, grate ginger, and chop cilantro.

2. Cook rice.

3. Cook chicken mixture.

Chicken with Asian Peanut Sauce

prep: 5 minutes • **cook:** 15 minutes   *POINTS* value: 8

Jasmine rice pairs exceptionally well with this saucy peanut-infused chicken, but you could also serve this dish over lo mein noodles.

  1 (8.5-ounce) package precooked jasmine rice (such as Uncle Ben's Ready Rice)
  ¼ cup reduced-fat peanut butter
  ¼ cup water
  2 tablespoons fresh lime juice
  2 tablespoons hoisin sauce
  1 teaspoon grated peeled fresh ginger
  2 teaspoons dark sesame oil
  1 pound chicken breast tenders
  ⅛ teaspoon salt
  ⅛ teaspoon black pepper
  3 tablespoons chopped fresh cilantro
  4 lime wedges

1. Microwave rice according to package directions.

2. Combine peanut butter, water, and next 3 ingredients in a small bowl, stirring with a whisk.

3. Heat oil in a large nonstick skillet over medium-high heat; add chicken. Sprinkle chicken with salt and pepper. Cook chicken 8 minutes, stirring occasionally, or until done. Add peanut sauce; cook 2 minutes or until thoroughly heated. Sprinkle with cilantro. Serve with lime wedges. **Yield:** 4 servings (serving size: ½ cup chicken mixture, about ⅓ cup rice, and 1 lime wedge).

Per serving: CALORIES 347 (29% from fat); FAT 11.2g (saturated fat 2g); PROTEIN 31.7g; CARBOHYDRATES 29.4g; FIBER 1.5g; CHOLESTEROL 66mg; IRON 2mg; SODIUM 371mg; CALCIUM 41mg

Hoisin-Glazed Chicken Thighs

prep: 7 minutes • **cook:** 12 minutes   *POINTS* value: 8

If you don't keep dry sherry on hand, substitute 1½ tablespoons water plus 1½ teaspoons cider vinegar for the sherry in this recipe.

  8 (3-ounce) skinless, boneless chicken thighs (about 1½ pounds)
Cooking spray
  ¼ cup hoisin sauce
  2 tablespoons dry sherry
  1 tablespoon grated peeled fresh ginger
  2 garlic cloves, pressed
  1 tablespoon toasted sesame seeds (such as McCormick)
  ¼ cup sliced green onions

1. Preheat broiler.
2. Place chicken thighs on a broiler pan coated with cooking spray. Combine hoisin sauce and next 3 ingredients in a small bowl, stirring well with a whisk. Remove and set aside 2 tablespoons sauce. Spoon 3 tablespoons sauce over chicken, spreading sauce with back of spoon; broil 6 minutes. Turn chicken. Spoon 3 tablespoons sauce over chicken; broil 6 minutes or until done.
3. Transfer chicken to a serving platter; brush with reserved 2 tablespoons sauce. Sprinkle with sesame seeds and green onions. Serve immediately. **Yield:** 4 servings (serving size: 2 thighs).

Per serving: CALORIES 324 (48% from fat); FAT 16.9g (saturated fat 4.2g); PROTEIN 31.4g; CARBOHYDRATES 8.4g; FIBER 0.5g; CHOLESTEROL 112mg; IRON 2mg; SODIUM 331mg; CALCIUM 44mg

Menu

POINTS value per serving: 8

Hoisin-Glazed Chicken Thighs

Fast Asian Slaw

Game Plan

1. While broiler heats:
  • Assemble chicken on pan; prepare sauce and spread over chicken.

2. While chicken cooks:
  • Prepare slaw.

Fast Asian Slaw

prep: 7 minutes   *POINTS* value: 0

  3 cups angel hair slaw
  1 cup finely shredded bok choy
  ½ cup thinly sliced green onions
  ⅓ cup chopped fresh cilantro
  ⅓ cup chopped fresh mint
  2 tablespoons rice vinegar
  1½ tablespoons less-sodium soy sauce (such as Kikkoman)
  1 teaspoon sesame oil
  ⅛ teaspoon salt
  ⅛ teaspoon freshly ground black pepper

1. Combine first 5 ingredients in a large bowl; toss well.
2. Combine vinegar, soy sauce, and sesame oil; pour over slaw, and toss to coat. Sprinkle with salt and pepper, tossing gently. **Yield:** 4 servings (serving size: 1 cup).

Per serving: CALORIES 36 (30% from fat); FAT 1.2g (saturated fat 0.2g); PROTEIN 1.3g; CARBOHYDRATES 4.7g; FIBER 1.9g; CHOLESTEROL 0mg; IRON 0.5mg; SODIUM 328mg; CALCIUM 35mg

Menu
POINTS value
per serving: 8

Sweet Mustard Chicken Thighs

Warm Balsamic Potato Salad

Game Plan

1. While grill heats:
  • Cook potatoes.
  • Prepare sauce; brush chicken with sauce.
  • Chop basil and roasted red bell peppers.
2. Cook chicken.
3. Toss salad.

Sweet Mustard Chicken Thighs

prep: 3 minutes • **cook:** 6 minutes   *POINTS* value: 7

These Carolina-style barbecue chicken thighs are smothered with a tangy-sweet sauce that will please the whole family.

½ cup prepared mustard
⅓ cup packed dark brown sugar
1 teaspoon ground allspice
¼ teaspoon crushed red pepper
8 (3-ounce) skinless, boneless chicken thighs (about 1½ pounds)
Cooking spray

1. Prepare grill.
2. Combine first 4 ingredients in a small bowl, stirring well. Reserve and set aside ¼ cup sauce mixture.
3. Place chicken on grill rack coated with cooking spray. Brush half of remaining ½ cup sauce mixture over 1 side of chicken. Grill chicken 3 to 4 minutes. Turn chicken over; brush with remaining half of sauce mixture. Cook 3 to 4 minutes or until done. Place chicken on a serving platter; drizzle with reserved ¼ cup sauce mixture. **Yield:** 4 servings (serving size: 2 thighs and 1 tablespoon sauce).

Per serving: CALORIES 317 (36% from fat); FAT 13g (saturated fat 3.6g); PROTEIN 30.5g; CARBOHYDRATES 18.3g; FIBER 0.3g; CHOLESTEROL 112mg; IRON 1.9mg; SODIUM 471mg; CALCIUM 34mg

Warm Balsamic Potato Salad

prep: 5 minutes • **cook:** 7 minutes   *POINTS* value: 1

½ pound mixed baby potatoes (such as fingerling, purple, and red), cut into wedges
1 tablespoon water
2 tablespoons light balsamic vinaigrette
¼ cup chopped bottled roasted red bell peppers
1 tablespoon chopped fresh basil
2 tablespoons crumbled goat cheese

1. Place potato wedges in a large microwave-safe bowl; add 1 tablespoon water. Cover with plastic wrap; vent (do not allow plastic wrap to touch food). Microwave at HIGH 7 minutes or until tender; drain.
2. Stir in vinaigrette, bell pepper, and basil. Top each serving with cheese.
Yield: 4 servings (serving size: about ⅓ cup potatoes and 1½ tablespoon cheese).

Per serving: CALORIES 67 (27% from fat); FAT 2g (saturated fat 0.9g); PROTEIN 1.9g; CARBOHYDRATES 10.2g; FIBER 1g; CHOLESTEROL 3mg; IRON 0.5mg; SODIUM 189mg; CALCIUM 17mg

Spicy Chicken Fajitas

prep: 7 minutes • **cook:** 8 minutes   ***POINTS*** value: 7

Simple to prepare and packed with flavor, this recipe is one you'll turn to every time you get a craving for sizzling Mexican fare. Serve with 1 tablespoon light sour cream or 1 tablespoon chopped avocado for an additional *POINTS* value of 1, if desired.

  6   skinless, boneless chicken thighs (about 1 pound)
  2   teaspoons fajita seasoning (such as McCormick)
Cooking spray
  2   cups vertically sliced onion
  2   cups red bell pepper strips
  4   (½-inch) 96% fat-free whole wheat tortillas, warmed
  ½   cup fresh salsa
Chopped avocado (optional)
Chopped fresh cilantro (optional)
Light sour cream (optional)

1. Cut chicken into ½-inch-wide strips. Place chicken in a small bowl; sprinkle with fajita seasoning, tossing to coat. Heat a large nonstick skillet over medium-high heat. Coat pan with cooking spray. Add chicken and onion; stir-fry 3 minutes. Add bell pepper; stir-fry 5 minutes or until chicken is done.
2. Place 1 tortilla on each of 4 plates. Top each evenly with chicken mixture and salsa. Top with avocado and cilantro, if desired. Fold tortillas over filling, and top with sour cream, if desired. Serve immediately. **Yield:** 4 servings (serving size: 1 tortilla, 1 cup chicken mixture, and 2 tablespoons salsa).

Per serving: CALORIES 341 (28% from fat); FAT 10.7g (saturated fat 2.4g); PROTEIN 25.4g; CARBOHYDRATES 34.8g; FIBER 4.6g; CHOLESTEROL 74mg; IRON 1.4mg; SODIUM 747mg; CALCIUM 27mg

Menu
POINTS value
per serving: 7

Spicy Chicken Fajitas

Game Plan

1. Cut onion and bell pepper.

2. Cut and season chicken.

3. While chicken cooks:
  • Warm tortillas.
  • Chop avocado and cilantro, if used.

pictured on page 113

Crunchy Oven-Fried Chicken

prep: 2 minutes • **cook:** 8 minutes

POINTS value: 7

Menu
POINTS value
per serving: 8

Crunchy Oven-Fried Chicken

Heirloom Tomato Salad

Game Plan

1. While oven preheats:
- Dredge chicken.
- Brown chicken.

2. While chicken bakes:
- Prepare salad.

⅓   cup fat-free buttermilk
2   tablespoons dill pickle juice
1   teaspoon seasoned salt
½   teaspoon freshly ground black pepper
4   (3-ounce) skinless chicken drumsticks
4   (3-ounce) skinless chicken thighs
1   cup panko (Japanese breadcrumbs)
1   tablespoon cornstarch
2   teaspoons canola oil
2   teaspoons butter

1. Preheat oven to 475°.
2. Combine first 4 ingredients in a large bowl; add chicken, tossing to coat. Combine panko and cornstarch in a large zip-top plastic bag.
3. Heat oil and butter in a large cast-iron skillet over medium-high heat until butter melts. Add chicken to panko mixture in bag; seal and shake well. Cook chicken in pan 3 to 4 minutes on each side or until brown. Place pan in oven; bake at 475° for 12 to 14 minutes or until chicken is done. **Yield:** 4 servings (serving size: 1 drumstick and 1 thigh).

Per serving: CALORIES 306 (32% from fat); FAT 10.9g (saturated fat 3g); PROTEIN 36.7g; CARBOHYDRATES 12.7g; FIBER 0.6g; CHOLESTEROL 141mg; IRON 1.8mg; SODIUM 392mg; CALCIUM 38mg

Heirloom Tomato Salad

prep: 7 minutes

POINTS value: 1

2   tablespoons white balsamic vinegar
1   teaspoon Dijon mustard
1   teaspoon minced shallots
1   garlic clove, pressed
¼   teaspoon salt
¼   teaspoon freshly ground black pepper
2   teaspoons extra-virgin olive oil
2   large heirloom tomatoes, cut into wedges (about 4 cups)
2   cups packed baby arugula leaves
¼   cup vertically sliced red onion
¼   cup packed small fresh basil leaves

1. Combine first 6 ingredients in a small bowl, stirring with a whisk. Add oil, whisking until blended.
2. Combine tomatoes, arugula, onion, and basil in a medium bowl. Pour dressing over tomato mixture, tossing gently to coat. **Yield:** 4 servings (serving size: 1½ cups).

Per serving: CALORIES 54 (43% from fat); FAT 2.6g (saturated fat 0.4g); PROTEIN 1.4g; CARBOHYDRATES 7.1g; FIBER 1.6g; CHOLESTEROL 0mg; IRON 0.6mg; SODIUM 185mg; CALCIUM 36mg

Turkey Cutlets with Balsamic–Brown Sugar Sauce

prep: 4 minutes • **cook:** 14 minutes   *POINTS* value: 7

     2   tablespoons all-purpose flour
    ½   teaspoon dried thyme
    ¼   teaspoon salt
    ¼   teaspoon freshly ground black pepper
    ¾   pound turkey cutlets (about 8 cutlets)
   2½   teaspoons olive oil, divided
     2   tablespoons thinly sliced shallots (1 medium)
    ⅓   cup dry red wine
    ⅓   cup fat-free, less-sodium chicken broth
     2   tablespoons balsamic vinegar
     1   tablespoon brown sugar
    ⅛   teaspoon salt

1. Combine first 4 ingredients in a shallow dish, stirring well with a whisk. Dredge turkey cutlets in flour mixture.

2. Heat 1½ teaspoons oil in a large nonstick skillet over medium-high heat. Cook cutlets 2 to 3 minutes on each side or until done. Remove cutlets from pan, and keep warm.

3. Heat remaining 1 teaspoon oil in pan over medium-high heat. Add shallots to pan, and sauté 1 minute. Stir in wine and broth, scraping pan to loosen browned bits. Bring to a boil; cook 5 minutes. Add vinegar, brown sugar, and ⅛ teaspoon salt. Bring to a boil; cook until sauce is reduced to ¼ cup (about 2 minutes). Serve over cutlets. **Yield:** 2 servings (serving size: ½ of cutlets and 2 tablespoons sauce).

Per serving: CALORIES 326 (18% from fat); FAT 6.5g (saturated fat 0.8g); PROTEIN 43.7g; CARBOHYDRATES 18.2g; FIBER 0.4g; CHOLESTEROL 68mg; IRON 3.3mg; SODIUM 695mg; CALCIUM 22mg

Sautéed Garlicky Spinach

prep: 2 minutes • **cook:** 4 minutes   *POINTS* value: 1

    ½   tablespoon olive oil
    1   garlic clove, thinly sliced
    1   (6-ounce) package baby spinach
    ⅛   teaspoon salt
    ⅛   teaspoon freshly ground black pepper

1. Heat oil in a large deep skillet or Dutch oven over medium heat. Add garlic; cook 1 minute or until golden. Add half of spinach; cook, 1 minute, turning with tongs. Add remaining half of spinach; cook 1 minute, turning with tongs, until spinach wilts. Stir in salt and pepper. **Yield:** 2 servings (serving size: ½ cup).

Per serving: CALORIES 54 (57% from fat); FAT 3.4g (saturated fat 0.5g); PROTEIN 2.2g; CARBOHYDRATES 3.8g; FIBER 2.1g; CHOLESTEROL 0mg; IRON 2.8mg; SODIUM 211mg; CALCIUM 85mg

---

Menu
POINTS value
per serving: 8

Turkey Cutlets with Balsamic–Brown Sugar Sauce

Sautéed Garlicky Spinach

Game Plan

1. Dredge turkey.

2. Cook turkey.

3. While sauce cooks:
   • Prepare spinach.

Turkey Cutlets with Cranberry-Cherry Sauce

prep: 2 minutes • **cook:** 14 minutes   *POINTS* value: 6

1½   pounds turkey cutlets
½   teaspoon salt
½   teaspoon freshly ground black pepper
1   tablespoon olive oil, divided
½   (12-ounce) container cranberry-orange crushed fruit (such as Ocean Spray Cran-Fruit)
¼   cup dried cherries
1½   teaspoons balsamic vinegar
½   teaspoon grated peeled fresh ginger

1. Sprinkle turkey with salt and pepper.
2. Heat 1½ teaspoons oil in a large nonstick skillet over medium-high heat. Add half of turkey, and cook 2 minutes on each side or until done. Remove turkey; keep warm. Repeat with remaining oil and turkey.
3. Add cranberry-orange crushed fruit and next 3 ingredients to pan. Bring mixture to a boil over medium-high heat. Return turkey to pan; nestle in cranberry-cherry sauce. Cover, reduce heat to medium-low, and simmer 3 minutes or until turkey is thoroughly heated. Remove cutlets from pan, and serve with cranberry-cherry sauce. **Yield:** 4 servings (serving size: about 2 cutlets and 3 tablespoons sauce).

Per serving: CALORIES 321 (12% from fat); FAT 4.3g (saturated fat 0.5g); PROTEIN 42.3g; CARBOHYDRATES 25.9g; FIBER 1.7g; CHOLESTEROL 68mg; IRON 2.4mg; SODIUM 449mg; CALCIUM 11mg

Roasted Brussels Sprouts à l'Orange

prep: 3 minutes • **cook:** 14 minutes   *POINTS* value: 1

2½   cups trimmed Brussels sprouts (about 8 ounces), halved lengthwise
2   teaspoons olive oil
¼   teaspoon salt
⅛   teaspoon black pepper
½   teaspoon grated fresh orange rind
2   tablespoons fresh orange juice

1. Preheat oven to 425°.
2. Place Brussels sprouts in a large bowl. Add oil, salt, and pepper; toss to coat. Place Brussels sprouts in a single layer on a foil-lined baking sheet. Roast at 425° for 7 minutes. Turn Brussels sprouts over, using a wide spatula. Bake an additional 7 minutes or until tender and browned.
3. Place Brussels sprouts in a bowl. Combine orange rind and juice, and drizzle over Brussels sprouts; toss well **Yield:** 4 servings (serving size: ⅔ cups).

Per serving: CALORIES 48 (45% from fat); FAT 2.4g (saturated fat 0.4g); PROTEIN 2g; CARBOHYDRATES 6g; FIBER 2.2g; CHOLESTEROL 0mg; IRON 0.8mg; SODIUM 160mg; CALCIUM 25mg

Crunchy Oven-Fried Chicken | page 110

Chicken Mozzarella and
Penne | page 105

Shrimp Salad with Avocado
and Grapefruit | page 131

Asian Chicken Salad
with Sweet and Spicy
Wasabi Dressing | page 135

BLT Steak Salad | page 134

Mile High Cheeseburger | page 152

Open-Faced Beef, Tomato, and
Pepperoncini Sandwich | page 151

Veggie Pitas with Cucumber Hummus | page 145

Potato-Bacon Soup | page 158

Corn and Bacon Chowder | page 157

Chorizo and Black Bean Soup | page 159

Blueberry Crumble Sundae | page 168

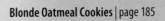

Blonde Oatmeal Cookies | page 185

Irish Cream Chocolate
Pudding Cakes | page 179

Chocolate-Hazelnut Mousse Cups | page 170

Blueberry-Lemon Cream Parfaits | page 169

Salads

Menu
POINTS value
per serving: 6

Mediterranean Tuna Salad

Greek-Style Pita Chips

Game Plan

1. While oven preheats:
- Separate and cut pitas; season pita wedges.
- Assemble pita wedges on pan.

2. While pita chips bake:
- Prepare salad.

3. Slice tomatoes, and top with tuna salad.

Mediterranean Tuna Salad

prep: 11 minutes   ***POINTS*** value: 4

This Mediterranean-style salad spotlights albacore tuna—a fish that is rich in omega-3 fatty acids. Serve the salad over sliced summer tomatoes with Greek-Style Pita Chips, or stuff the salad into 2 pita halves with shredded lettuce for lunch on the go with the same *POINTS* value per serving.

  1 (12-ounce) can albacore tuna in water, drained and flaked into large chunks
  ½ cup thinly sliced red onion
  2 celery stalks, thinly sliced
  2 tablespoons coarsely chopped pitted kalamata olives
2½ tablespoons fresh lemon juice
  1 tablespoon olive oil
  ¼ teaspoon freshly ground black pepper
  ⅛ teaspoon kosher salt
  2 large tomatoes, sliced

1. Combine first 4 ingredients in a medium bowl. Add lemon juice and next 3 ingredients; toss gently to combine. Serve salad over sliced tomatoes. **Yield:** 3 servings (serving size: 1 cup tuna salad and 2 tomato slices).

Per serving: CALORIES 203 (36% from fat); FAT 8g (saturated fat 1g); PROTEIN 24.9g; CARBOHYDRATES 9.1g; FIBER 2.3g; CHOLESTEROL 39mg; IRON 0.5mg; SODIUM 593mg; CALCIUM 31mg

Greek-Style Pita Chips

prep: 7 minutes • **cook:** 7 minutes   ***POINTS*** value: 2

  2 (6-inch) pitas
Olive oil–flavored cooking spray
  ½ teaspoon dried Greek seasoning

1. Preheat oven to 400°.
2. Cut each pita into 6 wedges. Separate each wedge into 2 triangles. Place triangles in a single layer on a large baking sheet. Coat top sides of triangles with cooking spray; sprinkle evenly with seasoning.
3. Bake at 400° for 7 to 8 minutes or until crisp and lightly browned; cool. **Yield:** 3 servings (serving size: 8 chips).

Per serving: CALORIES 107 (0% from fat); FAT 0g (saturated fat 0g); PROTEIN 4.7g; CARBOHYDRATES 22g; FIBER 0.7g; CHOLESTEROL 0mg; IRON 1.8mg; SODIUM 267mg; CALCIUM 27mg

pictured on page 115

Shrimp Salad with Avocado and Grapefruit

prep: 6 minutes   *POINTS* value: 6

Adding fresh lime juice to a bottled dressing gives it a "made from scratch" flavor. To save prep time, have your fishmonger peel and devein the shrimp. Or if you'd like to do it yourself, be sure to start with 1¼ pounds of unpeeled shrimp.

  1 (5-ounce) package mixed salad greens
  1 pound peeled cooked shrimp
  1 cup thinly sliced celery
  ⅓ cup light olive oil and vinegar dressing (such as Ken's Healthy Options)
  2 tablespoons fresh lime juice
  2 (8-ounce) containers red grapefruit sections, drained (such as Del Monte Fruit Naturals)
  1 peeled avocado, cut into 16 slices

1. Combine first 3 ingredients in a large bowl; toss gently. Combine dressing and lime juice, stirring with a whisk. Drizzle half of dressing mixture over salad mixture; toss well.
2. Divide salad evenly among 4 plates. Top salads evenly with grapefruit sections and avocado slices; drizzle salads evenly with remaining half of dressing mixture.
Yield: 4 servings (serving size: 2 cups salad, about ⅓ cup grapefruit sections, and 4 slices avocado).

Per serving: CALORIES 276 (38% from fat); FAT 11.7g (saturated fat 1.9g); PROTEIN 26.1g; CARBOHYDRATES 17.2g; FIBER 4.1g; CHOLESTEROL 221mg; IRON 4.8mg; SODIUM 461mg; CALCIUM 81mg

Menu
POINTS value
per serving: 7

Shrimp Salad with Avocado and Grapefruit

3 thin breadsticks
POINTS value: 1

Game Plan

1. Slice celery and avocado.

2. Prepare salad greens mixture.

3. Assemble salad.

Menu
POINTS value
per serving: 7

Tex-Mex Panzanella

1 orange
POINTS value: 1

Game Plan

1. While oven preheats:
• Cube corn bread.
• Drain and rinse black beans and corn.

2. While corn bread toasts:
• Prepare dressing.
• Chop tomato and cilantro.

3. Toss salad.

Tex-Mex Panzanella

prep: 5 minutes • **cook:** 10 minutes   *POINTS* value: 6

Panzanella is often thought of as a "leftover salad" and is usually made with leftover bread, fresh tomatoes, basil, olive oil, and vinegar. This version uses corn bread and has the ingredients and flavors of traditional Tex-Mex cuisine. Look for premade corn bread in the bakery at your supermarket. You can also serve this colorful salad over mixed greens.

      4   cups cubed corn bread (about 11 ounces)
      3   tablespoons fresh lime juice
      1   teaspoon ground cumin
     ¼   teaspoon salt
     ⅛   teaspoon black pepper
   1½   tablespoons canola oil
      1   (15-ounce) can black beans, rinsed and drained
      1   (11-ounce) can vacuum-packed reduced-sodium corn, drained
      1   large tomato, chopped
      1   cup (4 ounces) reduced-fat shredded sharp Cheddar cheese
     ¼   cup chopped fresh cilantro

1. Preheat oven to 400°.
2. Place corn bread on a large jelly-roll pan. Bake at 400° for 5 minutes; stir and bake an additional 5 minutes or until lightly browned.
3. While corn bread bakes, combine lime juice and next 3 ingredients in a large bowl, stirring with a whisk. Add oil, and stir with a whisk. Add beans, corn, and tomato; toss well. Add corn bread, cheese, and cilantro; toss gently. **Yield:** 6 servings (serving size: 1½ cups).

Per serving: CALORIES 289 (33% from fat); FAT 10.7g (saturated fat 3.8g); PROTEIN 10.6g; CARBOHYDRATES 39.9g; FIBER 4.6g; CHOLESTEROL 17mg; IRON 1.2mg; SODIUM 696mg; CALCIUM 173mg

Spinach, Tomato, and Fresh Mozzarella Pasta Salad with Italian Dressing

prep: 10 minutes • **cook:** 10 minutes   *POINTS* value: 6

Dressed with a simple vinaigrette made from fresh herbs and a good-quality extra-virgin olive oil, this salad is as delicious as it is easy to prepare. The dressing will keep in the refrigerator for a couple of days, so consider doubling the recipe to keep some on hand. Two tablespoons of the dressing has a *POINTS* value of 2 per serving.

2½ cups multigrain rotini pasta (such as Barilla PLUS)
¼ cup red wine vinegar
2 tablespoons chopped fresh flat-leaf parsley
1 tablespoon chopped fresh oregano or fresh basil
2 tablespoons extra-virgin olive oil
¼ teaspoon salt
¼ teaspoon freshly ground black pepper
2 garlic cloves, minced
2 cups grape tomatoes
1 (6-ounce) package baby spinach
4 ounces fresh mozzarella cheese, cubed

1. Cook pasta according to package directions, omitting salt and fat. Rinse with cold water; drain.
2. While pasta cooks, combine red wine vinegar and next 6 ingredients, stirring with a whisk. Combine dressing and tomatoes in a large bowl. Add pasta and spinach; toss well, and top with cheese. **Yield:** 4 servings (serving size: 1½ cups).

Per serving: CALORIES 300 (32% from fat); FAT 10.6g (saturated fat 3.4g); PROTEIN 13.3g; CARBOHYDRATES 38g; FIBER 5.3g; CHOLESTEROL 15mg; IRON 3.6mg; SODIUM 175mg; CALCIUM 173mg

Menu
POINTS value
per serving: 7

Spinach, Tomato, and
Fresh Mozzarella Pasta Salad
with Italian Dressing

1 cup strawberries
POINTS value: 1

Game Plan
1. While water for pasta comes to
a boil:
• Cube mozzarella.
• Chop herbs and mince garlic.

2. While pasta cooks:
• Combine ingredients for
Italian dressing.

3. Toss salad.

pictured on page 117

BLT Steak Salad

prep: 7 minutes • **cook:** 9 minutes • **other:** 5 minutes   *POINTS* value: 6

All of the high-flavor ingredients of a BLT sandwich are combined with beef tenderloin in this hearty, restaurant-quality salad. If 4-ounce steaks are hard to find, buy an 8-ounce steak from the meat case and cut it in half crosswise.

    4   precooked bacon slices
    2   (4-ounce) beef tenderloin steaks (about 1¼ inches thick), trimmed
    ½   teaspoon salt
    ½   teaspoon freshly ground black pepper
        Cooking spray
    6   cups torn romaine lettuce
    1   cup grape tomatoes, halved
    ½   cup light blue cheese dressing (such as Marie's)

1. Heat bacon according to package directions; crumble and set aside.
2. Sprinkle steaks evenly with salt and pepper; coat both sides with cooking spray.
3. Heat a medium nonstick skillet over medium-high heat. Add steaks; cook 4 to 5 minutes on each side or until desired degree of doneness. Remove steaks from pan; let stand 5 minutes. Cut each steak diagonally across grain into thin slices.
4. Combine lettuce, tomato, and sliced steak in a large bowl; toss well. Divide salad evenly among 4 plates; drizzle dressing evenly over salads. Sprinkle with crumbled bacon. **Yield:** 4 servings (serving size: 2 cups salad, 1½ ounces steak, 2 tablespoons dressing, and 1 tablespoon crumbled bacon).

Per serving: CALORIES 243 (53% from fat); FAT 14.2g (saturated fat 4.1g); PROTEIN 20.6g; CARBOHYDRATES 8g; FIBER 2.3g; CHOLESTEROL 57mg; IRON 2mg; SODIUM 772mg; CALCIUM 86mg

---

Menu
POINTS value
per serving: 8

BLT Steak Salad

1 (1-ounce) dinner roll
POINTS value: 2

Game Plan

1. While bacon cooks and oven preheats for rolls:
• Season steak.

2. While steak cooks:
• Tear lettuce and halve grape tomatoes.
• Warm rolls in oven.

3. Toss salad.

pictured on page 116

Asian Chicken Salad with Sweet and Spicy Wasabi Dressing

prep: 10 minutes

POINTS value: 7

Don't be shy about using the wasabi powder—the dressing is full of flavor, not heat. Rotisserie chicken works well for this salad, although any shredded cooked chicken will do.

2	tablespoons rice vinegar
2	tablespoons maple syrup
2	tablespoons olive oil
¾	teaspoon wasabi powder (dried Japanese horseradish)
¼	teaspoon salt
⅛	teaspoon freshly ground black pepper
1	(11.4-ounce) package Asian supreme salad mix (such as Fresh Express)
1	(8¼-ounce) can mandarin oranges in light syrup, drained
2	cups shredded cooked chicken breast (about ¾ pound)
1	diagonally cut green onion

1. Combine first 6 ingredients in a large bowl; stir well with a whisk.
2. Add salad mix to vinegar mixture, reserving wonton strips for topping and sesame-orange dressing for another use. Add oranges and chicken; toss gently to coat. Top evenly with green onions and reserved wonton strips. **Yield:** 4 servings (serving size: about 1½ cups salad and 3 wonton strips).

Per serving: CALORIES 316 (40% from fat); FAT 14g (saturated fat 3.6g); PROTEIN 25.3g; CARBOHYDRATES 23.5g; FIBER 2.5g; CHOLESTEROL 67mg; IRON 1.5mg; SODIUM 279mg; CALCIUM 100mg

Menu
POINTS value
per serving: 7

Asian Chicken Salad with Sweet and Spicy Wasabi Dressing

Game Plan

1. Prepare salad dressing.

2. Drain oranges, shred chicken, and slice green onion.

3. Toss salad.

Menu
POINTS value
per serving: 8

Chop Cobb Salad

½ cup lemon sorbet
POINTS value: 2

Game Plan

1. Cube bread.

2. While bread bakes:
  • Chop eggs.
  • Rinse and drain chickpeas.
  • Prepare dressing.

3. Assemble salad.

4. Scoop sorbet into bowls.

Chop Cobb Salad

prep: 8 minutes • **cook:** 12 minutes • **other:** 2 minutes   **POINTS** value: 6

Homemade bread cubes, which bake in the oven while you prepare the other ingredients, are worth the extra effort—though you may use commercial fat-free croutons instead.

    4   ounces whole-grain Italian bread, cut into ½-inch cubes
Cooking spray
    5   hard-cooked large eggs
    1   (12-ounce) package American-style mixed salad greens (such as
        Fresh Express)
    1   (16-ounce) can chickpeas (garbanzo beans), rinsed and drained
    1   cup prechopped green bell pepper
    ½   cup prechopped red onion
    ½   cup light ranch dressing (such as Naturally Fresh)
    ⅓   cup (1.3 ounces) crumbled blue cheese
Freshly ground black pepper

1. Arrange bread cubes in a single layer on a large baking sheet; lightly coat bread cubes with cooking spray. Place baking sheet in oven while preheating to 350°. Bake bread cubes 12 minutes or until firm. Remove from oven, and cool 2 minutes.
2. While bread cubes bake, cut eggs in half lengthwise; remove and reserve 3 yolks for another use. Chop remaining egg whites and yolks.
3. Combine chopped egg, salad greens, and next 3 ingredients in a large bowl. Add bread cubes; toss gently. Divide salad evenly among 5 plates. Combine dressing and cheese in a small bowl. Drizzle evenly over each salad; toss well. Sprinkle with freshly ground black pepper. **Yield:** 5 servings (serving size: about 2 cups salad and about 1½ tablespoons dressing).

Per serving: CALORIES 291 (34% from fat); FAT 11g (saturated fat 2.9g); PROTEIN 13.4g; CARBOHYDRATES 33.4g; FIBER 5.7g; CHOLESTEROL 85mg; IRON 2.9mg; SODIUM 688mg; CALCIUM 147mg

Curried Chicken-Rice Salad

prep: 8 minutes • **cook:** 4 minutes • **other:** 8 minutes   *POINTS* value: 5

Crisp Gala apple and crunchy celery give this nutrient-rich salad an extra dimension of tantalizing texture and color. An excellent source of vitamin C, celery helps strengthen the immune system.

1   (10-ounce) package frozen microwavable brown rice (such as Birds Eye)
1   cup vanilla fat-free yogurt
1   teaspoon curry powder
¼   teaspoon salt
3   cups chopped cooked chicken breast (about 1 pound)
1½   cups chopped Gala apple (about 1 medium)
½   cup chopped celery
¼   cup cherry-flavored sweetened dried cranberries (such as Craisins)
     Green leaf lettuce leaves (optional)

1. Prepare rice according to package directions. Spread rice in a shallow pan; place in freezer 8 to 10 minutes.
2. While rice chills, combine yogurt, curry powder, and salt in a large bowl. Add chicken and next 3 ingredients to yogurt mixture, stirring until coated.
3. Stir chilled rice into chicken mixture. Spoon chicken salad onto lettuce leaves, if desired. **Yield:** 6 servings (serving size: 1 cup).

Per serving: CALORIES 238 (11% from fat); FAT 3g (saturated fat 0.8g); PROTEIN 25.3g; CARBOHYDRATES 26.5g; FIBER 1.9g; CHOLESTEROL 60mg; IRON 1mg; SODIUM 187mg; CALCIUM 97mg

Menu
POINTS value
per serving: 6

Curried Chicken-Rice Salad

1 cup red grapes
POINTS value: 1

Game Plan

1. While rice cooks:
• Chop chicken.

2. While rice chills:
• Chop apple and celery.
• Prepare dressing.

3. Toss salad.

Menu

POINTS value
per serving: 6

**Grilled Chicken and Romaine
Salad with Raspberry Vinaigrette**

Grilled Garlic Bread

Game Plan

1. While grill preheats:
- Halve romaine hearts.
- Toast almonds.
- Halve garlic.

2. Grill chicken, romaine hearts, and bread.

3. Assemble salad.

Grilled Chicken and Romaine Salad with Raspberry Vinaigrette

prep: 7 minutes • **cook:** 4 minutes   **POINTS** value: 4

  8 (2-ounce) chicken cutlets
Olive oil–flavored cooking spray
¼ teaspoon salt
¼ teaspoon freshly ground black pepper
  2 hearts of romaine, halved lengthwise
½ cup fat-free raspberry vinaigrette, divided
½ cup fresh raspberries
¼ cup prechopped green onions
¼ cup sliced almonds, toasted

1. Prepare grill.
2. Coat chicken with cooking spray; sprinkle with salt and pepper.
3. Place chicken and romaine halves on grill rack coated with cooking spray; brush chicken evenly with ¼ cup vinaigrette. Grill chicken and romaine 2 to 3 minutes on each side or until chicken is done and lettuce is lightly charred. Slice chicken into thin strips.
4. Diagonally cut romaine halves in half, and place evenly on 4 plates. Top evenly with sliced chicken, raspberries, green onions, toasted almonds, and remaining ¼ cup vinaigrette. **Yield:** 4 servings (serving size: 1 romaine half, 3 ounces chicken, 2 tablespoons berries, 1 tablespoon green onions, 1 tablespoon almonds, and 1 tablespoon vinaigrette).

Per serving: CALORIES 224 (23% from fat); FAT 5.6g (saturated fat 0.7g); PROTEIN 29g; CARBOHYDRATES 14g; FIBER 4.1g; CHOLESTEROL 66mg; IRON 2.3mg; SODIUM 519mg; CALCIUM 71mg

Grilled Garlic Bread

prep: 2 minutes • **cook:** 4 minutes   **POINTS** value: 2

  4 (0.7-ounce) Italian bread slices
  1 garlic clove, halved
  2 teaspoons extra-virgin olive oil
Cooking spray

1. Prepare grill.
2. Rub bread slices with cut sides of garlic halves; brush evenly with oil. Place bread slices on grill rack coated with cooking spray. Grill 2 minutes on each side or until lightly toasted. **Yield:** 4 servings (serving size: 1 slice).

Per serving: CALORIES 75 (36% from fat); FAT 3g (saturated fat 0.5g); PROTEIN 1.8g; CARBOHYDRATE 10.2g; FIBER 0.6g; CHOLESTEROL 0mg; IRON 0.6mg; SODIUM 116mg; CALCIUM 17mg

Sandwiches

Louisiana Catfish Po' Boy

**Herbed Tomato-
Cucumber Salad**

Game Plan

1. While oven preheats:
  • Prepare vegetables for salad.
  • Season and dredge catfish.

2. While catfish cooks:
  • Prepare coleslaw.
  • Prepare dressing for salad;
    toss with vegetables.

3. Assemble sandwiches.

Louisiana Catfish Po' Boys

prep: 6 minutes • **cook:** 9 minutes   ***POINTS*** value: 6

    4 (3-ounce) catfish fillets
  Cooking spray
    1 teaspoon Creole seasoning (such as Tony Chachere's)
    1 cup cornflakes, coarsely crushed
    2 teaspoons olive oil
    3 cups 3-color coleslaw (such as Fresh Express)
    3 tablespoons light mayonnaise
    3 tablespoons chopped green onions (about 1)
    2 tablespoons prepared horseradish
    2 teaspoons Creole mustard
    2 teaspoons water
    4 (1.5-ounce) white wheat hot dog buns (such as Nature's Own)
    4 lemon wedges

1. Preheat oven to 425°. Place a large baking sheet in oven while oven preheats.
2. Coat fish with cooking spray. Sprinkle fish with Creole seasoning; recoat with cooking spray. Dredge fish in cornflake crumbs.
3. Spread olive oil on hot baking sheet. Add fish. Bake at 425° for 9 minutes or until fish flakes easily when tested with a fork. Cut fish in half lengthwise.
4. While fish bakes, combine coleslaw and next 5 ingredients in a bowl; toss well.
5. Place 1 fillet on bottom of each bun. Top each with ¾ cup coleslaw mixture and a bun top. Serve with lemon wedges. **Yield:** 4 servings (serving size: 1 sandwich and 1 lemon wedge).

Per serving: CALORIES 304 (42% from fat); FAT 14.1g (saturated fat 2.6g); PROTEIN 19.7g; CARBOHYDRATES 30.4g; FIBER 6.2g; CHOLESTEROL 43mg; IRON 4.2mg; SODIUM 6mg; CALCIUM 297mg

Herbed Tomato-Cucumber Salad

prep: 6 minutes   ***POINTS*** value: 1

    1 tablespoon olive oil
    2 teaspoons champagne vinegar
    ½ teaspoon minced garlic
    ¼ teaspoon salt
    ¼ teaspoon Italian seasoning
    ⅛ teaspoon black pepper
    2 medium tomatoes, cut into wedges
    1 cup cucumber slices
    ¼ cup diced sweet onion

1. Combine first 6 ingredients in a medium bowl, stirring with a whisk. Stir in remaining ingredients. Serve immediately. **Yield:** 4 servings (serving size: ¾ cup).

Per serving: CALORIES 51 (64% from fat); FAT 3.6g (saturated fat 0.5g); PROTEIN 0.9g; CARBOHYDRATES 4.6g; FIBER 1.1g; CHOLESTEROL 0mg; IRON 0.3mg; SODIUM 150mg; CALCIUM 14mg

Open-Faced Smoked Salmon Sandwiches with Dill Cream Cheese Spread

prep: 12 minutes • **cook:** 2 minutes   *POINTS* value: 3

Served with a mixed green salad, this light salmon sandwich is perfect for a warm summer's day. Low in calories and rich in protein, alfalfa sprouts crown this sandwich with lots of vitamins and minerals—particularly vitamin C.

¼   cup (2 ounces) tub-style light chive-and-onion cream cheese
2   teaspoons chopped fresh dill
2   teaspoons capers, rinsed
4   (1-ounce) slices pumpernickel bread, toasted
4   ounces thinly sliced smoked salmon
8   (¼-inch-thick) slices red onion
1   cup alfalfa sprouts

1. Combine first 3 ingredients in a bowl, stirring until well blended.
2. Spread 1 tablespoon cream cheese mixture over each of 4 bread slices. Top each with 1 ounce salmon, 2 onion slices, and ¼ cup sprouts. **Yield:** 4 servings (serving size: 1 sandwich).

Per serving: CALORIES 176 (24% from fat); FAT 5g (saturated fat 1.9g); PROTEIN 10.7g; CARBOHYDRATES 23.6g; FIBER 3.6g; CHOLESTEROL 14mg; IRON 1.4mg; SODIUM 568mg; CALCIUM 66mg

Pomegranate Refreshers

prep: 4 minutes   *POINTS* value: 1

2   cups pomegranate juice, chilled
¼   cup fresh lemon juice
3   tablespoons sugar
2   cups club soda, chilled
Ice cubes
Lemon slices (optional)

1. Combine first 3 ingredients in a small pitcher, stirring until sugar dissolves. Gently stir in club soda. Serve over ice, and garnish with lemon slices, if desired. **Yield:** 6 servings (serving size: about ¾ cup).

Per serving: CALORIES 73 (0% from fat); FAT 0g (saturated fat 0g); PROTEIN 0.4g; CARBOHYDRATES 18.8g; FIBER 0g; CHOLESTEROL 0mg; IRON 0.1mg; SODIUM 27mg; CALCIUM 18mg

Menu
POINTS value
per serving: 4

Open-Faced Smoked Salmon Sandwich with Dill Cream Cheese Spread

Pomegranate Refresher

1 cup mixed green salad with fat-free balsamic vinaigrette
POINTS value: 0

Game Plan

1. Combine juices and sugar for Pomegranate Refreshers; slice lemon, if desired.

2. While bread toasts:
  • Prepare cream cheese spread.

3. Assemble sandwiches.

4. Toss salad.

5. Add club soda to juice mixture; pour over ice.

Menu
POINTS value
per serving: 8

**Southwestern Shrimp
and Bacon Club**

**1 cup sliced
kiwifruit and pineapple**
POINTS value: 1

Game Plan

1. Season shrimp.

2. While shrimp cook:
- Microwave bacon.
- Slice tomatoes.
- Slice fruit.

3. Assemble sandwiches.

Southwestern Shrimp and Bacon Club

prep: 5 minutes • **cook:** 6 minutes

POINTS value: 7

Look for "top loading" hot dog rolls, instead of the traditional rolls that are stuffed from the side, in the deli or bread section of your grocery store.

- ¾ pound peeled and deveined medium shrimp
- Cooking spray
- 1½ teaspoons salt-free Southwest chipotle seasoning (such as Mrs. Dash)
- 8 slices precooked bacon
- 4 slices tomato, cut in half
- 4 (2.1-ounce) wheat hot dog rolls (such as Toufayan Snuggles)
- 1 cup shredded iceberg lettuce
- ¼ cup light ranch dressing (such as Naturally Fresh)

1. Coat shrimp with cooking spray; sprinkle with seasoning.

2. Heat a large nonstick skillet over medium-high heat. Add shrimp, and sauté 5 minutes or until shrimp are done.

3. Microwave bacon slices according to package directions.

4. Place 2 tomato slice halves in each roll; top with ¼ cup lettuce and 2 slices bacon. Top each with one-fourth of shrimp; drizzle 1 tablespoon dressing over each sandwich. **Yield:** 4 servings (serving size: 1 sandwich).

Per serving: CALORIES 347 (33% from fat); FAT 12.6g (saturated fat 3g); PROTEIN 25.7g; CARBOHYDRATES 33.2g; FIBER 3.6g; CHOLESTEROL 139mg; IRON 3.3mg; SODIUM 588mg; CALCIUM 81mg

Meatless Muffuletta

prep: 20 minutes

POINTS value: 6

Muffuletta sandwiches are typically a meat-lover's dream, but this one is a meatless surprise. No one will ever suspect that it's a vegetarian version.

- 1   (16-ounce) package frozen broccoli, cauliflower, and carrots, thawed and chopped
- 3   tablespoons white wine vinegar
- ½   cup chopped bottled roasted red bell peppers
- 3   tablespoons light olive oil vinaigrette (such as Ken's)
- 3   tablespoons chopped fresh flat-leaf parsley
- 3   garlic cloves, minced
- 2   tablespoons chopped pitted manzanilla (or green) olives
- 2   tablespoons chopped ripe olives
- ½   teaspoon freshly ground black pepper
- 1   (18-ounce) loaf Italian bread
- 1   (5.5-ounce) package meatless deli salami (such as Yves)
- 4   (¾-ounce) slices reduced-fat Havarti cheese
- 4   (¾-ounce) slices part-skim mozzarella cheese

1. Combine chopped broccoli mixture and vinegar; toss well. Set aside.

2. Combine bell peppers and next 6 ingredients in a large bowl; toss well.

3. Hollow out top and bottom of loaf, leaving a 1-inch-thick shell; reserve torn bread for another use.

4. Drain broccoli mixture; add to bell pepper mixture. Spoon half of bell pepper mixture into bottom half of loaf. Arrange salami and cheeses on top of bell pepper mixture; top with remaining bell pepper mixture and top half of loaf. Press down firmly with hands. Wrap loaf with plastic wrap; refrigerate until ready to serve. Cut sandwich into 5 pieces. **Yield:** 5 servings (serving size: 1 sandwich slice).

Per serving: CALORIES 284 (30% from fat); FAT 9.5g (saturated fat 3.9g); PROTEIN 21.6g; CARBOHYDRATES 26.2g; FIBER 3.3g; CHOLESTEROL 20mg; IRON 3.5mg; SODIUM 965mg; CALCIUM 210mg

Menu
POINTS value per serving: 6

Meatless Muffuletta

1 cup grape tomatoes
POINTS value: 0

Game Plan

1. While broccoli thaws in microwave:
- Chop red bell peppers, parsley, garlic, and olives.

2. Chop broccoli mixture and stir in vinegar.

3. Prepare red bell pepper mixture.

4. Hollow out bread.

5. Assemble sandwich.

Pesto Grilled Cheese Sandwiches

prep: 3 minutes • **cook:** 17 minutes

POINTS value: 8

With a new take on a familiar favorite, this adult grilled cheese sandwich is loaded with Italian flavors and toasted until golden brown. Save any leftover pesto to toss with pasta, or use it to add a distinct herbal flavor to fish or chicken.

    4   teaspoons reduced-fat commercial pesto (such as Buitoni)
    8   (1-ounce) slices sourdough bread
    8   (¾-ounce) slices part-skim mozzarella cheese
    4   (¼-inch-thick) slices tomato
    1   tablespoon olive oil

1. Spread 1 teaspoon pesto on each bread slice; top each of 4 bread slices with 1 cheese slice, 1 tomato slice, 1 additional cheese slice, and a remaining bread slice, pesto side down.

2. Heat oil in a large nonstick skillet over medium-low heat. Add sandwiches in batches; cook 4 minutes on each side or until golden and cheese melts.

Yield: 4 servings (serving size: 1 sandwich).

Per serving: CALORIES 345 (38% from fat); FAT 14.6g (saturated fat 6.4g); PROTEIN 18.3g; CARBOHYDRATES 33.4g; FIBER 1.8g; CHOLESTEROL 25mg; IRON 1.9mg; SODIUM 599mg; CALCIUM 346mg

pictured on page 120

Veggie Pitas with Cucumber Hummus

prep: 15 minutes

POINTS value: 5

Make extra hummus to serve as a snack with vegetables or pita chips; 2 tablespoons has a *POINTS* value of 1 per serving. For convenience, prepare the hummus up to three days in advance and refrigerate in an airtight container.

Menu
POINTS value
per serving: 6

Veggie Pita with Cucumber Hummus

1 cup red grapes
POINTS value: 1

Game Plan

1. Rinse and drain chickpeas.

2. Slice cucumber, tomatoes, and onion.

3. Process hummus.

4. Assemble pitas.

1	(16-ounce) can chickpeas (garbanzo beans), rinsed and drained
¾	cup sliced English cucumber
¼	cup lightly packed fresh mint leaves
¼	cup lightly packed fresh parsley leaves
2	tablespoons fresh lemon juice
½	teaspoon salt
½	teaspoon freshly ground black pepper
1	(8-ounce) package pita halves (such as Salad Pockets)
3	romaine lettuce leaves, cut in half
2	plum tomatoes, sliced
¾	cup matchstick-cut carrots
½	cup sliced red onion

1. Combine first 7 ingredients in a blender or food processor; process until smooth.

2. Spread ¼ cup hummus in each pita half. Place ½ lettuce leaf in each pita half. Top evenly with tomato slices, carrots, and red onion. Serve immediately. **Yield:** 3 servings (serving size: 2 pita halves).

Per serving: CALORIES 291 (7% from fat); FAT 2.2g (saturated fat 0.5g); PROTEIN 11.4g; CARBOHYDRATES 56g; FIBER 11.9g; CHOLESTEROL 0mg; IRON 2.2mg; SODIUM 808mg; CALCIUM 65mg

Menu
POINTS value
per serving: 8

Chicken Sandwich with White Barbecue Sauce

Melon Salad

Game Plan

1. Prepare salad.

2. Prepare barbecue sauce.

3. Assemble sandwiches.

Chicken Sandwiches with White Barbecue Sauce

prep: 5 minutes   *POINTS* value: 7

White barbecue sauce, widely used in Alabama-style barbecue, is known for its vinegary taste and its use of mayonnaise as its base, rather than the usual tomato sauce.

- ½   cup low-fat mayonnaise
- ⅓   cup cider vinegar
- 1   tablespoon fresh lemon juice
- 1½ teaspoons freshly ground black pepper
- ⅛   teaspoon ground red pepper
- 2   cups packaged angel hair slaw
- 6   (1.8-ounce) white wheat hamburger buns
- 3   cups shredded rotisserie chicken
- 12 hamburger dill pickle slices

1. Combine first 5 ingredients in a small bowl, stirring with a whisk.

2. Place ⅓ cup slaw on bottom half of each bun; top each with ½ cup chicken, about 2 tablespoons barbecue sauce, 2 pickle slices, and a bun top. **Yield:** 6 servings (serving size: 1 sandwich).

Per serving: CALORIES 379 (20% from fat); FAT 8.6g (saturated fat 2g); PROTEIN 52.3g; CARBOHYDRATES 25.5g; FIBER 5.7g; CHOLESTEROL 129mg; IRON 1.6mg; SODIUM 653mg; CALCIUM 332mg

Melon Salad

prep: 9 minutes   *POINTS* value: 1

- 4   cups cubed seeded watermelon
- 1½   cups cubed peeled honeydew melon
- 1½   cups cubed peeled cantaloupe
- ¼   cup fresh lime juice (about 2 limes)
- 2   tablespoons chopped fresh mint
- 2   tablespoons honey

1. Combine first 3 ingredients in a large bowl.

2. Combine lime juice, mint, and honey in a small bowl, stirring with a whisk. Drizzle over fruit; toss gently to coat. Cover and chill until ready to serve. **Yield:** 6 servings (serving size: about 1 cup).

Per serving: CALORIES 84 (0% from fat); FAT 0g (saturated fat 0g); PROTEIN 1.3g; CARBOHYDRATES 21.5g; FIBER 1g; CHOLESTEROL 0mg; IRON 0.5mg; SODIUM 16mg; CALCIUM 16mg

Cobb Salad Sandwiches

prep: 10 minutes • **cook:** 2 minutes   ***POINTS*** value: 5

Cobb salads are traditionally loaded with high-fat items such as bacon, blue cheese, and avocado. Here we use all these yummy ingredients in smaller amounts to create a flavorful, calorie-friendly version of the sandwich.

¼ cup refrigerated light chunky blue cheese dressing (such as Marie's)
1 tablespoon ready-to-serve real bacon bits (such as Oscar Mayer)
1 cup bagged torn romaine lettuce
4 (1.6-ounce) multigrain sandwich thins (such as Arnold), toasted
8 ounces thinly sliced lemon pepper–flavored deli chicken breast (such as Boar's Head)
½ avocado, thinly sliced
¼ cup thinly sliced red onion

1. Combine blue cheese dressing and bacon bits in a small bowl; set aside.
2. Place ¼ cup torn lettuce on each bottom half of sandwich thins. Top lettuce evenly with chicken, avocado slices, and onion. Spoon dressing mixture evenly over onion. Cover with top halves of sandwich thins. **Yield:** 4 servings (serving size: 1 sandwich).

Per serving: CALORIES 253 (33% from fat); FAT 9.2g (saturated fat 3.2g); PROTEIN 18.4g; CARBOHYDRATES 30g; FIBER 9.1g; CHOLESTEROL 38mg; IRON 2mg; SODIUM 737mg; CALCIUM 69mg

Menu
POINTS value
per serving: 8

Cobb Salad Sandwich

1 ounce reduced-fat baked kettle chips (about 23)
POINTS value: 3

Game Plan

1. Prepare dressing.

2. While bread toasts:
• Slice avocado and onion.

3. Assemble sandwiches.

Menu
POINTS value
per serving: 8

Turkey Reuben Wrap

Carrot Slaw

Game Plan

1. Prepare slaw.

2. While pan heats:
• Rinse and drain sauerkraut.

3. While caraway seeds toast:
• Prepare mayonnaise mixture.

4. Assemble wraps.

Turkey Reuben Wraps

prep: 10 minutes • **cook:** 4 minutes   *POINTS* value: 7

Adding toasted caraway seeds to the sauerkraut gives these wraps an interesting flavor boost.

    1   teaspoon caraway seeds
    ⅔   cup sauerkraut, rinsed and drained
    3   tablespoons light mayonnaise
    2   tablespoons ketchup
    1   tablespoon Dijon mustard
    1   tablespoon sweet pickle relish
    4   (8-inch) fat-free whole wheat tortillas (such as Olé Mexican Foods)
    6   ounces sliced deli lower-sodium turkey breast (such as Boar's Head)
    4   (1-ounce) slices reduced-fat Swiss cheese (such as Alpine Lace)

1. Heat a small skillet over medium-high heat. Add caraway seeds, and cook 2 minutes or until toasted, stirring frequently. Combine caraway seeds and sauerkraut in a small bowl; set aside.

2. Combine mayonnaise and next 3 ingredients in a small bowl; stir well with a whisk.

3. Spread about 1½ tablespoons mayonnaise mixture on each tortilla. Divide turkey evenly among tortillas; top each with 1 cheese slice. Top cheese evenly with sauerkraut mixture. Roll up; secure with wooden picks, if necessary. Place wraps on a microwave-safe plate; cover with a damp paper towel. Microwave at HIGH 2 minutes or until cheese melts. **Yield:** 4 servings (serving size: 1 wrap).

Per serving: CALORIES 317 (32% from fat); FAT 11.4g (saturated fat 4.3g); PROTEIN 21.7g; CARBOHYDRATES 30g; FIBER 1.9g; CHOLESTEROL 39mg; IRON 1.4mg; SODIUM 962mg; CALCIUM 326mg

Carrot Slaw

prep: 5 minutes   *POINTS* value: 1

    4   teaspoons fresh lemon juice
    1½   teaspoons olive oil
    1½   teaspoons honey
    ⅛   teaspoon freshly ground black pepper
    1/16 teaspoon salt
    1¾   cups grated carrot
    ¾   cup diced Granny Smith apple

1. Combine first 5 ingredients in a medium bowl, stirring with a whisk. Add carrot and apple; toss well. **Yield:** 4 servings (serving size: about ½ cup).

Per serving: CALORIES 57 (28% from fat); FAT 1.8g (saturated fat 0.3g); PROTEIN 0.6g; CARBOHYDRATES 11g; FIBER 1.7g; CHOLESTEROL 0mg; IRON 0.2mg; SODIUM 70mg; CALCIUM 18mg

Mediterranean Turkey Burgers with Red Bell Pepper Mayo

prep: 8 minutes • **cook:** 10 minutes

POINTS value: 8

Feta cheese, kalamata olives, and capers give these juicy burgers a Greek accent.

1	pound lean ground turkey breast
1	large egg white
⅓	cup (1.3 ounces) crumbled feta cheese
¼	cup dry breadcrumbs
3	tablespoons chopped pitted kalamata olives
1	tablespoon capers, minced
½	teaspoon dried oregano
¼	teaspoon freshly ground black pepper
	Cooking spray
3	tablespoons light mayonnaise
2	tablespoons minced bottled roasted red bell peppers, drained
4	(1.5-ounce) white wheat hamburger buns, toasted
4	green leaf lettuce leaves
4	slices tomato
4	slices red onion

1. Combine first 8 ingredients in a large bowl; stir until blended. Divide mixture into 4 equal portions, shaping each into a ½-inch-thick patty.

2. Heat a large nonstick skillet over medium heat. Coat pan with cooking spray. Place patties in pan; cook 5 to 6 minutes on each side or until done.

3. While burgers cook, combine mayonnaise and bell peppers in a small bowl. Spread mayonnaise mixture on both halves of each bun. Place 1 patty on bottom half of each bun; top with 1 lettuce leaf, 1 tomato slice, 1 red onion slice, and top half of bun. **Yield:** 4 servings (serving size: 1 burger).

Per serving: CALORIES 380 (44% from fat); FAT 18.5g (saturated fat 5.9g); PROTEIN 31.7g; CARBOHYDRATES 27.1g; FIBER 5.3g; CHOLESTEROL 86mg; IRON 4.2mg; SODIUM 766mg; CALCIUM 342mg

---

Menu
POINTS value
per serving: 8

Mediterranean Turkey Burger with Red Bell Pepper Mayo

1 cup squash and zucchini strips
POINTS value: 0

Game Plan

1. Prepare patties.

2. While burgers cook:
- Prepare mayonnaise mixture.
- Slice tomato and onion.
- Cut squash and zucchini.

3. Assemble burgers.

Steak and Mint Pesto Wraps

prep: 7 minutes • **cook:** 13 minutes   ***POINTS*** value: 7

Menu
POINTS value
per serving: 8

Steak and Mint Pesto Wrap

1 cup precubed watermelon
POINTS value: 1

Game Plan

1. While grill preheats:
• Slice onion.
• Season steak.

2. While steak and onion cook:
• Prepare pesto.
• Warm tortillas.

3. Assemble wraps.

You'll have about ¼ cup extra pesto so plan to serve it with grilled lamb or pork. A serving size of 1 tablespoon has a *POINTS* value of 2.

    1   pound flank steak, trimmed
    ½   teaspoon kosher salt
    ½   teaspoon freshly ground black pepper
    ½   large red onion, cut into ½-inch-thick slices
    Cooking spray
  1½   cups fresh mint leaves
    ½   cup fresh flat-leaf parsley leaves
    ¼   cup (1 ounce) preshredded Parmesan cheese
    1   tablespoon coarsely chopped walnuts
    1   tablespoon extra-virgin olive oil
    1   tablespoon fresh lemon juice
    1   tablespoon water
    1   garlic clove, halved
    4   (8-inch) low-carb flour tortillas (such as Mission Carb Balance)
    ¼   cup (1 ounce) crumbled goat cheese

1. Prepare grill.

2. Sprinkle steak on both sides with salt and pepper. Coat steak and onion with cooking spray, and place on grill rack. Grill 13 minutes or until steak is desired degree of doneness and onion is tender, turning after 6 minutes. Remove steak and onion from grill; cover and keep warm.

3. While steak and onion cook, place mint and next 7 ingredients in a food processor; process until smooth, scraping sides of bowl occasionally.

4. Warm tortillas according to package directions. Cut steak diagonally across grain into thin slices. Spread 1 tablespoon pesto on each tortilla, reserving remaining pesto for another use. Arrange sliced beef and onion evenly in center of each tortilla; sprinkle evenly with goat cheese. Roll up, and serve immediately. **Yield:** 4 servings (serving size: 1 wrap).

Per serving: CALORIES 345 (35% from fat); FAT 13.6g (saturated fat 4.8g); PROTEIN 33g; CARBOHYDRATES 22.9g; FIBER 12.4g; CHOLESTEROL 43mg; IRON 3.6mg; SODIUM 723mg; CALCIUM 195mg

pictured on page 119

Open-Faced Beef, Tomato, and Pepperoncini Sandwiches

prep: 12 minutes • **cook:** 6 minutes   *POINTS* value: 5

Mixed greens tossed with assertive feta cheese, tangy pepperoncini peppers, and savory seared flank steak piled high on top of toasted sourdough bread make this recipe a salad and sandwich in one. Use a knife and fork to eat this hearty dish.

4	(1.5-ounce) slices sourdough bread
½	pound flank steak, trimmed
⅛	teaspoon salt
⅛	teaspoon freshly ground black pepper
	Cooking spray
2	cups grape tomatoes, halved
1	cup packed mixed baby greens
½	cup drained and chopped pepperoncini peppers
1	tablespoon extra-virgin olive oil
1½	tablespoons chopped fresh oregano
1	garlic clove, minced
¼	cup (1 ounce) crumbled feta cheese

1. Toast bread slices; set aside.
2. While bread toasts, sprinkle steak with salt and pepper. Heat a large nonstick skillet over medium-high heat until hot. Coat pan with cooking spray. Add steak; cook 3 to 4 minutes on each side or until desired degree of doneness. Cut steak diagonally across grain into very thin slices.
3. While steak cooks, combine tomatoes and next 6 ingredients in a medium bowl.
4. Place 1 bread slice on each of 4 plates. Top evenly with tomato mixture and steak. **Yield:** 4 servings (serving size: 1 sandwich).

Per serving: CALORIES 259 (34% from fat); FAT 9.9g (saturated fat 3.1g); PROTEIN 18.5g; CARBOHYDRATES 25.4g; FIBER 2.6g; CHOLESTEROL 27mg; IRON 3.2mg; SODIUM 608mg; CALCIUM 126mg

---

Menu
POINTS value
per serving: 7

Open-Faced Beef, Tomato, and Pepperoncini Sandwich

½ cup strawberry sorbet
POINTS value: 2

Game Plan

1. While bread toasts:
• Halve tomatoes.
• Season steak.

2. While steak cooks:
• Prepare tomato mixture.

3. Assemble sandwiches.

4. Scoop sorbet into serving bowls.

pictured on page 118

Mile High Cheeseburger

prep: 4 minutes • **cook:** 13 minutes   ***POINTS*** value: 8

These old-fashioned, onion ring–topped cheeseburgers get a flavor boost from Worcestershire sauce, grated onion, and garlic powder. All they need is to be dressed with your favorite toppings and condiments. For an additional ***POINTS*** value of 2, serve this juicy burger with 3 ounces of oven-baked steak fries (about 7).

  8 frozen onion rings (such as Alexia)
  1 pound ground sirloin
  1 tablespoon grated onion
  1 tablespoon Worcestershire sauce
  1 teaspoon garlic powder
  ¼ teaspoon salt
  ¼ teaspoon freshly ground black pepper
  Cooking spray
  4 (0.7-ounce) slices reduced-fat sharp Cheddar cheese
  4 (1.75-ounce) white wheat hamburger buns
  Lettuce leaves, tomato slices, ketchup, and mustard (optional)

1. Prepare grill.
2. Preheat oven to 450°.
3. Bake onion rings at 450° for 10 minutes; turn over, and bake an additional 3 to 4 minutes or until golden and crisp.
4. While onion rings bake, combine beef and next 5 ingredients. Shape mixture into 4 (½-inch-thick) patties.
5. Place patties on grill rack coated with cooking spray. Grill 3 to 4 minutes on each side or until done. Top with cheese slices; grill 1 minute or just until cheese melts.
6. While cheese melts, place buns, cut sides down, on grill rack. Grill 1 minute or until toasted. Place cheeseburgers on bottom halves of buns; top with onion rings and bun tops, adding lettuce, tomato slices, ketchup, and mustard, if desired. **Yield:** 4 servings (serving size: 1 burger).

Per serving: CALORIES 367 (36% from fat); FAT 14.5g (saturated fat 5.3g); PROTEIN 34.2g; CARBOHYDRATES 32.8g; FIBER 5.9g; CHOLESTEROL 71mg; IRON 2.1mg; SODIUM 656mg; CALCIUM 452mg

---

Menu
POINTS value
per serving: 8

Mile High Cheeseburger

1 cup garden salad
with red wine vinaigrette
POINTS value: 0

Game Plan

1. While grill and oven preheat:
• Prepare patties.

2. While onion rings bake:
• Grill burgers.
• Toss salad.

3. Assemble burgers.

Soups

Thai Fish Soup

prep: 5 minutes • **cook:** 10 minutes　　　　***POINTS*** value: 4

In this creamy soup, the delicately flavored seafood is infused with the authentic Thai seasonings of cilantro, ginger, and lemongrass. Boil the edamame pods in salted water for 3 to 5 minutes, drain, and then cool on a baking sheet for a few minutes. To eat the edamame, use your thumb and forefinger to squeeze the beans from the pod into your mouth and discard the pods.

2　(14-ounce) cans light coconut milk
1　(14-ounce) can fat-free, less-sodium chicken broth
1　cup water
2　tablespoons grated peeled fresh ginger
1　tablespoon minced fresh lemongrass
2　tablespoons lime juice
1　tablespoon fish sauce
2　teaspoons chili paste
¼　pound bay scallops
¼　pound peeled and deveined medium shrimp
¼　pound halibut or other lean white fish, cut into 1-inch pieces
3　green onions, chopped
2　tablespoons chopped fresh cilantro

1. Combine first 8 ingredients in a Dutch oven; cover and bring to a boil. Reduce heat; add scallops and next 3 ingredients. Simmer 3 minutes or until thoroughly cooked. Ladle soup into bowls, and top with cilantro. **Yield:** 6 servings (serving size: 1⅓ cups).

Per serving: CALORIES 129 (47% from fat); FAT 6.7g (saturated fat 5.9g); PROTEIN 12.5g; CARBOHYDRATES 7.4g; FIBER 0.3g; CHOLESTEROL 42mg; IRON 1.3mg; SODIUM 571mg; CALCIUM 22mg

Quick Tortellini-Spinach Soup

prep: 4 minutes • **cook:** 11 minutes   ***POINTS*** value: 3

Buy a package of baby spinach to save preparation time; its tender leaves require no trimming or chopping. Pour the leftover soup in small portable containers to pack for tomorrow's lunch.

   3   (14-ounce) cans fat-free, less-sodium chicken broth
1½ tablespoons chopped fresh basil
   1   teaspoon minced garlic
   1   (9-ounce) package fresh cheese tortellini
   2   cups fresh baby spinach
   1   cup chopped tomato
  ½ cup sliced green onions (about 3 onions)
  ¼ cup (1 ounce) preshredded Parmesan cheese

1. Combine first 3 ingredients in a large saucepan; cover and bring to a boil. Add tortellini; reduce heat, and simmer, uncovered, 5 minutes. Remove from heat; stir in spinach, tomato, and green onions. Ladle into bowls, and sprinkle with cheese; serve immediately. **Yield:** 7 servings (serving size: 1 cup soup and about ½ tablespoon cheese).

Per serving: CALORIES 145 (20% from fat); FAT 3.3g (saturated fat 1.7g); PROTEIN 9g; CARBOHYDRATES 20.5g; FIBER 1.9g; CHOLESTEROL 16mg; IRON 1.1mg; SODIUM 656mg; CALCIUM 101mg

Greens with Strawberries and Pomegranate Dressing

prep: 6 minutes • **cook:** 2 minutes   ***POINTS*** value: 3

   1   (5-ounce) package gourmet salad greens
   2   cups quartered strawberries
  ¾ cup thinly sliced red onion
  ⅓ cup sliced almonds, toasted
   1   teaspoon poppy seeds
  ¼ cup pomegranate juice
   2   tablespoons sugar
   2   tablespoons red wine vinegar
   1   tablespoon canola oil

1. Layer first 4 ingredients in a large bowl; sprinkle with poppy seeds.
2. Combine juice and next 3 ingredients in a jar. Cover tightly; shake vigorously. Drizzle dressing over salad; toss well. Serve immediately. **Yield:** 4 servings (serving size: about 2 cups).

Per serving: CALORIES 156 (45% from fat); FAT 7.8g (saturated fat 0.6g); PROTEIN 3.1g; CARBOHYDRATES 20.7g; FIBER 3.9g; CHOLESTEROL 0mg; IRON 1.1mg; SODIUM 17mg; CALCIUM 52mg

---

Menu
POINTS value
per serving: 6

Quick Tortellini-Spinach Soup

Greens with Strawberries and Pomegranate Dressing

Game Plan

1. Chop basil and mince garlic.

2. While broth mixture comes to a boil:
  • Chop tomato and onions.
  • Quarter strawberries and slice red onion.

3. While soup simmers:
  • Toast almonds.
  • Prepare dressing.

4. Toss salad.

Quick Corn and Beef Chili

prep: 2 minutes • **cook:** 18 minutes

POINTS value: 5

This recipe has the flavor of a chili that has simmered all day—only you will know that it hasn't. Look for precooked corn bread in the bakery at your supermarket.

Cooking spray
1 pound 93% lean ground beef
¼ teaspoon black pepper
1 (8-inch) 96% fat-free flour tortilla (such as Mission Heart Healthy)
1¾ cups frozen whole-kernel corn
1 (14.5-ounce) can no-salt-added diced tomatoes, undrained
1½ cups chunky bottled salsa (such as Pace)
1 tablespoon adobo sauce

1. Preheat oven to 425°.

2. Heat a 4-quart saucepan over medium-high heat. Coat pan with cooking spray. Add beef and black pepper to pan; cook 10 minutes or until browned, stirring to crumble.

3. While beef cooks, cut tortilla into thin strips (about 2 inches long). Coat tortilla strips with cooking spray, and spread in a single layer on a baking sheet. Bake at 425° for 5 to 7 minutes or until golden.

4. Add corn and next 3 ingredients to beef mixture; cover and bring to a boil. Reduce heat, and cook 5 minutes or until thoroughly heated, stirring occasionally. Ladle chili into bowls; top evenly with tortilla strips. **Yield:** 5 servings (serving size: 1 cup chili and ⅕ of tortilla strips).

Per serving: CALORIES 245 (27% from fat); FAT 7.3g (saturated fat 2.5g); PROTEIN 19.2g; CARBOHYDRATES 27g; FIBER 5.7g; CHOLESTEROL 44mg; IRON 3.2mg; SODIUM 798mg; CALCIUM 36mg

pictured on page 122

Corn and Bacon Chowder

prep: 2 minutes • **cook:** 14 minutes   ***POINTS*** value: 4

To capture the freshness of yellow jewel-like corn without the fuss of shucking ears or cutting kernels off the cob, use packages of frozen baby gold and white corn. This chowder is so wonderfully sweet with the frozen corn that our taste testers gave it our highest rating. Thaw the corn quickly by placing it in a colander under running water until thawed.

- 2   bacon slices
- ½   cup refrigerated prechopped celery, onion, and bell pepper mix
- 2   (16-ounce) packages frozen baby gold and white corn, thawed and divided
- 2   cups 1% low-fat milk, divided
- ½   teaspoon salt
- ¼   teaspoon freshly ground black pepper
- ¾   cup (3 ounces) reduced-fat shredded extra-sharp Cheddar cheese (such as Cracker Barrel)
- Freshly ground black pepper (optional)

1. Cook bacon in a Dutch oven over medium heat until crisp. Remove bacon from pan; crumble and set aside. Add celery mixture and 1 package corn to drippings in pan; sauté 5 minutes or until vegetables are tender.

2. Place remaining 1 package corn and 1 cup milk in a blender, and process until smooth. Add pureed mixture to vegetables in pan; stir in remaining 1 cup milk, salt, black pepper, and cheese. Cook over medium heat (do not boil), stirring constantly, until cheese melts. Ladle chowder into bowls. Top each serving evenly with reserved crumbled bacon. Sprinkle with additional black pepper, if desired. **Yield:** 6 servings (serving size: 1 cup).

Per serving: CALORIES 215 (24% from fat); FAT 6g (saturated fat 3.1g); PROTEIN 10.8g; CARBOHYDRATES 33.6g; FIBER 3.8g; CHOLESTEROL 15mg; IRON 0.8mg; SODIUM 402mg; CALCIUM 208mg

Tomato, Avocado, and Onion Salad

prep: 7 minutes   ***POINTS*** value: 1

- 3   small heirloom tomatoes, sliced
- ½   Vidalia or other sweet onion, vertically thinly sliced
- ½   cup coarsely chopped ripe peeled avocado (about ½ avocado)
- 1½   tablespoons thinly sliced fresh basil
- 2   tablespoons light Northern Italian salad dressing with basil and Romano (such as Ken's Steak House Lite)

1. Combine first 4 ingredients in a large bowl, tossing gently. Drizzle dressing evenly over salad; toss gently to coat. **Yield:** 6 servings (serving size: about ¾ cup).

Per serving: CALORIES 46 (57% from fat); FAT 3g (saturated fat 0.3g); PROTEIN 0.9g; CARBOHYDRATES 5g; FIBER 1.5g; CHOLESTEROL 0mg; IRON 0.3mg; SODIUM 61mg; CALCIUM 16mg

---

Menu
POINTS value
per serving: 5

Corn and Bacon Chowder

Tomato, Avocado, and Onion Salad

Game Plan

1. While bacon cooks:
- Thaw corn.
- Prepare salad.

2. Sauté celery and corn.

3. Blend corn and milk.

4. Cook soup.

pictured on page 121

Potato-Bacon Soup

prep: 1 minute • **cook:** 19 minutes   ***POINTS*** value: 5

To prepare this recipe in 20 minutes from start to finish, measure the potatoes and chop the onion and parsley while the bacon cooks.

2 center-cut bacon slices (uncooked), cut into ½-inch pieces
¾ cup chopped onion (1 small)
4 cups frozen Southern-style hash brown potatoes (such as Ore-Ida)
1 (14-ounce) can fat-free, less-sodium chicken broth
¼ teaspoon salt
⅛ teaspoon freshly ground black pepper
1 cup 1% low-fat milk
2 tablespoons chopped green onions
½ cup (2 ounces) reduced-fat shredded extra-sharp Cheddar cheese (such as Cracker Barrel)

1. Cook bacon in a large saucepan over medium heat 2 minutes, stirring frequently; add onion. Cook, stirring frequently, 5 minutes or until bacon is crisp.
2. Add potatoes to bacon mixture, stirring to coat with bacon drippings. Add broth, salt, and pepper; cover and bring to a boil over high heat, stirring frequently. Boil 6 minutes, stirring frequently. Mash potatoes with a potato masher until soup is slightly thick. Stir in milk. Cook, stirring constantly, 1 minute or until thoroughly heated; remove from heat. Ladle soup into bowls; sprinkle evenly with green onions and cheese. **Yield:** 4 servings (serving size: 1 cup).

Per serving: CALORIES 225 (38% from fat); FAT 9.4g (saturated fat 0.7g); PROTEIN 11.9g; CARBOHYDRATES 24.4g; FIBER 1.6g; CHOLESTEROL 30mg; IRON 0.2mg; SODIUM 812mg; CALCIUM 235mg

---

Menu
POINTS value
per serving: 7

Potato-Bacon Soup

1 (1-ounce) baguette slice, toasted
POINTS value: 2

Game Plan

1. While oven for toast heats:
• Assemble baguette slices on baking sheet.
• Chop onion for bacon mixture.
• Cook bacon mixture.

2. While soup cooks:
• Toast bread.
• Chop green onions.

pictured on page 123

Chorizo and Black Bean Soup

prep: 7 minutes • **cook:** 10 minutes   *POINTS* value: 4

Chorizo, a Spanish pork sausage, kicks up the heat in this dish. If you'd like, add a squeeze of fresh lime juice to enhance the bold flavors of this hearty soup.

Cooking spray
1⅓ cups chopped green bell pepper (1 large)
  2 (4-ounce) fresh chorizo links, casings removed
  1 cup chopped onion
  2 garlic cloves, minced
  3 cups fat-free, less-sodium chicken broth
  2 (15-ounce) cans black beans, rinsed and drained
  1 (14.5-ounce) can diced tomatoes, undrained
  3 tablespoons no-salt-added tomato paste
  2 teaspoons ground cumin
  ½ cup chopped fresh cilantro

1. Heat a large saucepan over medium heat. Coat pan with cooking spray. Add bell pepper and next 3 ingredients; cook 5 minutes or until chorizo is browned, stirring to crumble.
2. Stir in broth and next 4 ingredients; cover and cook over high heat 5 minutes, stirring often. Remove pan from heat; stir in cilantro. **Yield:** 8 servings (serving size: 1 cup).

Per serving: CALORIES 216 (47% from fat); FAT 11.3g (saturated fat 4.1g); PROTEIN 13g; CARBOHYDRATES 17.8g; FIBER 5.6g; CHOLESTEROL 25mg; IRON 2.1mg; SODIUM 793mg; CALCIUM 44mg

---

Menu
POINTS value
per serving: 7

Chorizo and Black Bean Soup

1 ounce tortilla chips (about 12)
POINTS value: 3

Game Plan

1. Chop bell pepper and onion; mince garlic.

2. Remove casings from chorizo.

3. Cook chorizo mixture.

4. Simmer soup.

Menu
POINTS value
per serving: 8

Chicken-and-Rice Soup with Avocado and Pico de Gallo

Fresh Lime and Oregano Spring Greens Salad

Game Plan

1. While broth mixture comes to a boil:
- Mince garlic and oregano.
- Juice lime.

2. While soup simmers:
- Prepare pico de gallo.
- Prepare salad.

Chicken-and-Rice Soup with Avocado and Pico de Gallo

prep: 4 minutes • **cook:** 16 minutes   *POINTS* value: 6

Pico de gallo, a fresh relish made primarily of chopped tomato, onion, and jalapeño, transforms a traditionally mild chicken-and-rice soup into a lively weeknight supper.

  1 (32-ounce) carton fat-free, less-sodium chicken broth
  1 (3½-ounce) bag boil-in-bag long-grain rice
  1¼ cups shredded cooked chicken breast
  ¼ teaspoon black pepper
  1¼ cups finely chopped seeded tomato
  ⅓ cup prechopped onion
  ¼ cup chopped fresh cilantro
  2 tablespoons minced pickled jalapeño peppers
  2 tablespoons fresh lime juice
  ¼ teaspoon salt
  1 diced peeled avocado

1. Bring broth to a boil in a Dutch oven. Remove rice from bag, and stir into broth. Add chicken and black pepper; cover, reduce heat, and simmer 10 minutes or until rice is tender.
2. While rice cooks, combine tomato and next 5 ingredients in a small bowl; stir well.
3. Ladle soup into bowls; top evenly with avocado and tomato mixture. **Yield:** 4 servings (serving size: 1 cup soup, ¼ avocado, and about ½ cup tomato mixture).

Per serving: CALORIES 272 (31% from fat); FAT 9.4g (saturated fat 1.7g); PROTEIN 20.4g; CARBOHYDRATES 29.1g; FIBER 3.5g; CHOLESTEROL 37mg; IRON 2mg; SODIUM 857mg; CALCIUM 23mg

Fresh Lime and Oregano Spring Greens Salad

prep: 7 minutes   *POINTS* value: 2

  1 garlic clove, minced
  2 tablespoons water
  1½ tablespoons extra-virgin olive oil
  1 tablespoon fresh lime juice
  1 teaspoon chopped fresh oregano
  ¼ teaspoon freshly ground black pepper
  ⅛ teaspoon salt
  1 (5-ounce) package spring greens

1. Combine first 7 ingredients in a large bowl; stir well with a whisk. Add greens, and toss gently to coat. **Yield:** 4 servings (serving size: about 1 cup).

Per serving: CALORIES 70 (84% from fat); FAT 7g (saturated fat 1.4g); PROTEIN 1.3g; CARBOHYDRATES 2.1g; FIBER 0.6g; CHOLESTEROL 3mg; IRON 0.2mg; SODIUM 171mg; CALCIUM 38mg

Southwestern Chicken and White Bean Soup

prep: 2 minutes • **cook:** 18 minutes   ***POINTS*** value: 3

Fresh cilantro adds an extra zing of flavor and a bright burst of color to this dish. For a nonalcoholic version of the fruit salad, substitute 3 additional tablespoons grapefruit juice for the rum.

    2   cups shredded cooked chicken breast
    1   tablespoon 40%-less-sodium taco seasoning (such as Old El Paso)
    Cooking spray
    2   (14-ounce) cans fat-free, less-sodium chicken broth
    1   (16-ounce) can cannellini beans or other white beans, rinsed and drained
    ½   cup green salsa
    Light sour cream (optional)
    Chopped fresh cilantro (optional)

1. Combine chicken and taco seasoning; toss well to coat. Heat a large saucepan over medium-high heat. Coat pan with cooking spray. Add chicken; sauté 2 minutes or until chicken is lightly browned. Add broth, scraping pan to loosen browned bits.

2. Place beans in a small bowl; mash until only a few whole beans remain. Add beans and salsa to pan, stirring well. Bring to a boil. Reduce heat; simmer 10 minutes or until slightly thick. Serve with sour cream and cilantro, if desired. **Yield:** 6 servings (serving size: 1 cup).

Per serving: CALORIES 134 (19% from fat); FAT 3g (saturated fat 0.5g); PROTEIN 18g; CARBOHYDRATES 8.5g; FIBER 1.8g; CHOLESTEROL 40mg; IRON 1.1mg; SODIUM 623mg; CALCIUM 22mg

Spirited Tropical Fruit Salad

prep: 7 minutes • **cook:** 2 minutes   ***POINTS*** value: 3

    1   (24-ounce) jar ruby red grapefruit sections
    3   tablespoons light brown sugar
    3   tablespoons dark rum
    2   cups fresh pineapple chunks
    3   kiwifruit, peeled and cut into wedges
    ¼   cup flaked sweetened coconut, toasted

1. Drain grapefruit sections, reserving 2 tablespoons juice. Combine reserved juice, brown sugar, and rum in a medium bowl, stirring well. Add grapefruit sections, pineapple, and kiwifruit. Toss gently. Serve immediately, or cover and chill. Sprinkle with toasted coconut before serving. **Yield:** 4 servings (serving size: 1 cup fruit, 1 tablespoon coconut, and 2 tablespoons juice).

Per serving: CALORIES 203 (2% from fat); FAT 1.8g (saturated fat 1.3g); PROTEIN 2.2g; CARBOHYDRATES 41.3g; FIBER 3.9g; CHOLESTEROL 0mg; IRON 0.8mg; SODIUM 27mg; CALCIUM 57mg

---

Menu
POINTS value
per serving: 6

Southwestern Chicken and White Bean Soup

Spirited Tropical Fruit Salad

Game Plan

1. While chicken mixture cooks:
  • Rinse and drain beans.

2. While soup simmers:
  • Prepare salad.

Menu
POINTS value
per serving: 7

Spicy Sausage, White Bean,
and Spinach Soup

Asiago-Topped Garlic Bread

Game Plan

1. While oven preheats and broth mixture comes to a boil:
- Rinse and drain beans.
- Slice sausage.

2. While soup simmers:
- Chop spinach.
- Prepare bread.

3. Stir spinach into soup.

Spicy Sausage, White Bean, and Spinach Soup

prep: 1 minute • **cook:** 16 minutes   **POINTS** value: 4

Andouille is a spicy smoked sausage that is often used in Cajun dishes like jambalaya and gumbo.

  1 (14-ounce) can fat-free, less-sodium chicken broth
  1 (14.5-ounce) can fire-roasted diced tomatoes, undrained
  1 (15-ounce) can no-salt-added navy beans, drained
  2 (3-ounce) links fully cooked andouille sausage (such as Aidell's), thinly sliced
  3 cups packed fresh baby spinach, coarsely chopped

1. Bring broth and tomatoes to a boil in a medium saucepan over high heat. Add beans and sausage; bring to a boil. Cook, uncovered, 8 minutes or until thoroughly heated. Stir in spinach; cook 1 minute or until spinach wilts. **Yield:** 4 servings (serving size: about 1⅓ cups).

Per serving: CALORIES 198 (29% from fat); FAT 6.3g (saturated fat 2.3g); PROTEIN 14.6g; CARBOHYDRATES 21.2g; FIBER 6.5g; CHOLESTEROL 25mg; IRON 3.2mg; SODIUM 910mg; CALCIUM 96mg

Asiago-Topped Garlic Bread

prep: 6 minutes • **cook:** 4 minutes   **POINTS** value: 3

   1 garlic clove, pressed
   1 (6-ounce) whole wheat French bread baguette, cut in half lengthwise
 1½ tablespoons light olive oil vinaigrette
  ½ teaspoon chopped fresh rosemary
  ¼ cup (1 ounce) finely grated Asiago cheese

1. Preheat broiler.
2. Spread garlic on cut sides of bread; brush evenly with vinaigrette. Top evenly with rosemary and cheese.
3. Broil 4 minutes or until cheese melts and bread is lightly browned. Cut into 8 pieces. **Yield:** 4 servings (serving size: 2 pieces).

Per serving: CALORIES 138 (22% from fat); FAT 3g (saturated fat 1.4g); PROTEIN 5.6g; CARBOHYDRATES 20.2g; FIBER 0.7g; CHOLESTEROL 7mg; IRON 1.1mg; SODIUM 283mg; CALCIUM 70mg

Desserts

Italian Berry Float

prep: 5 minutes

POINTS value: 4

This refreshing dessert is ideal for celebrating the start of summer. You can use any sparkling white wine, but we prefer the crispness of Italian Prosecco.

2   cups blood orange or lemon sorbet
2   cups mixed berries (such as raspberries, strawberries, blackberries, and blueberries)
2   cups Prosecco or other sparkling wine
    Mint sprigs

1. Place ½ cup sorbet in each of 4 glasses. Arrange ½ cup berries evenly around sorbet in each glass. Pour ½ cup Prosecco over berries in each glass; garnish with mint sprigs. Serve immediately. **Yield:** 4 servings (serving size: 1 float).

Per serving: CALORIES 203 (1% from fat); FAT 0.3g (saturated fat 0g); PROTEIN 0.6g; CARBOHYDRATES 30.4g; FIBER 2.7g; CHOLESTEROL 0mg; IRON 0.4mg; SODIUM 34mg; CALCIUM 13mg

Peppermint Candy–Cone–Crunch Ice Cream

prep: 8 minutes

POINTS value: 5

Enjoy an ice-cream cone and peppermint crunch in every bite of this ice-cream parlor–style treat!

2	cups vanilla fat-free ice cream (such as Edy's), slightly softened
¼	cup fat-free hot fudge topping
¼	cup mini chocolate chips
¼	cup crushed soft peppermints
2	sugar cones, slightly crushed

1. Combine all ingredients in a large bowl; spoon into dessert dishes. Serve immediately, or scoop into a freezer-safe container; cover and freeze. **Yield:** 5 servings (serving size: about ½ cup).

Per serving: CALORIES 239 (13% from fat); FAT 3.5g (saturated fat 2.1g); PROTEIN 4.7g; CARBOHYDRATES 47.2g; FIBER 1.7g; CHOLESTEROL 0mg; IRON 0.4mg; SODIUM 96mg; CALCIUM 97mg

Chocolate Chip Ice-Cream Balls

prep: 10 minutes • **other:** 1 hour

POINTS value: 5

Who would have thought fiber could be so yummy? Try experimenting with other whole wheat and rice cereals (such as 75%-less-sugar Cinnamon Toast Crunch).

1½   cups caramel-flavored lightly sweetened crunchy whole wheat squares (such as Fiber One Caramel Delight), coarsely crushed
3   tablespoons semisweet chocolate minichips
2   cups vanilla fat-free ice cream (such as Edy's)
¼   cup fat-free caramel topping (such as Smucker's)

1. Combine crushed whole wheat cereal and minichips in a shallow dish.
2. Scoop out ice cream, ½ cup at a time, and shape into 4 balls. Roll balls in cereal mixture, pressing gently to coat. Place on a shallow dish; freeze 1 hour or until firm. Place 1 ball on each of 4 serving dishes; drizzle each ball with 1 tablespoon caramel topping. **Yield:** 4 servings (serving size: 1 ice-cream ball).

Per serving: CALORIES 251 (13% from fat); FAT 3.6g (saturated fat 1.4g); PROTEIN 4.5g; CARBOHYDRATES 55.5g; FIBER 6.9g; CHOLESTEROL 0mg; IRON 2.1mg; SODIUM 209mg; CALCIUM 50mg

Chocolate–Peanut Butter Shake

prep: 6 minutes

POINTS value: 3

A little peanut butter goes a long way to provide flavor and creamy texture in this thick shake.

   3   cups chocolate fat-free ice cream
   ¾   cup fat-free milk
   1   tablespoon creamy peanut butter
   2   teaspoons unsweetened cocoa
   ½   teaspoon vanilla extract

1. Combine all ingredients in a blender; process until smooth, scraping sides. Serve immediately. **Yield:** 4 servings (serving size: ¾ cup).

Per serving: CALORIES 178 (11% from fat); FAT 2.2g (saturated fat 0.5g); PROTEIN 7.2g; CARBOHYDRATES 36.7g; FIBER 6.6g; CHOLESTEROL 1mg; IRON 1.3mg; SODIUM 121mg; CALCIUM 209mg

pictured on page 124

Blueberry Crumble Sundae

prep: 4 minutes • **cook:** 15 minutes   *POINTS* value: 6

With its buttery crumb topping and rich fruit filling, this decadent sundae is reminiscent of a classic homemade blueberry crumble.

  1   (21-ounce) can blueberry pie filling (such as Lucky Leaf)
Cooking spray
  ½   cup all-purpose flour
  3   tablespoons light brown sugar
  ¼   cup sliced almonds
  2   tablespoons butter, softened
  3   cups vanilla fat-free ice cream (such as Edy's)

1. Preheat oven to 375°.
2. Spread pie filling in a 2-quart baking dish coated with cooking spray; set aside.
3. Lightly spoon flour into a dry measuring cup; level with a knife. Combine flour, brown sugar, and almonds in a small bowl. Cut in butter with a pastry blender or 2 knives until mixture resembles coarse meal. Sprinkle flour mixture over pie filling. Coat top with cooking spray.
4. Bake at 375° for 15 minutes or until topping is lightly browned and pie filling is bubbly. Serve with ice cream. **Yield:** 6 servings (serving size: ½ cup ice cream and ½ cup blueberry mixture).

Per serving: CALORES 305 (17% from fat); FAT 5.9g (saturated fat 2.6g); PROTEIN 5g; CARBOHYDRATES 58.3g; FIBER 1.9g; CHOLESTEROL 10mg; IRON 0.7mg; SODIUM 74mg; CALCIUM 96mg

pictured on page 128

Blueberry-Lemon Cream Parfaits

prep: 6 minutes

POINTS value: 4

In these parfaits, lemon curd combined with cream cheese and ice cream forms a custardlike sauce. Substitute sliced strawberries for the blueberries, or use both for a variation.

- ¼ cup (2 ounces) block-style ⅓-less-fat cream cheese
- 2 tablespoons lemon curd
- ¾ cup vanilla light ice cream, slightly softened (such as Edy's)
- 1 teaspoon grated lemon rind
- ½ cup coarsely crushed sugar-free shortbread cookies (about 12 cookies; such as Murray's)
- 1 cup blueberries

1. Place cream cheese and lemon curd in a small bowl; beat with a mixer at medium-high speed until smooth. Add ice cream and lemon rind; beat well.

2. Spoon 1 tablespoon cookie crumbs into each of 4 glasses. Top each with 2 tablespoons cream cheese mixture and 2 tablespoons blueberries. Repeat procedure once. Serve immediately. **Yield:** 4 servings (serving size: 1 parfait).

Per serving: CALORIES 183 (35% from fat); FAT 7.1g (saturated fat 3.6g); PROTEIN 3.7g; CARBOHYDRATES 27.7g; FIBER 2.4g; CHOLESTEROL 24.3mg; IRON 0.4mg; SODIUM 142mg; CALCIUM 53mg

pictured on page 127

Chocolate-Hazelnut Mousse Cups

prep: 19 minutes • **cook:** 1 minute • **other:** 2 hours   *POINTS* value: 3

Don't tell anyone there's tofu in this rich make-ahead dessert. Chances are they'll never guess. Frangelico is a sweet hazelnut-flavored liqueur that contains hints of cacao, vanilla, coffee, and toasted hazelnut. A bottle of Frangelico keeps indefinitely and is certainly worth the price.

  2 (12.3-ounce) packages reduced-fat firm silken tofu
     (such as Mori-Nu Lite)
  ½ cup sugar
  6 tablespoons unsweetened cocoa
  2 tablespoons Frangelico (hazelnut-flavored liqueur)
  ½ teaspoon vanilla extract
Dash of salt
  ⅓ cup dark chocolate chips (such as Hershey's Special Dark)
 18 chocolate graham crackers (4½ cookie sheets)
  9 tablespoons frozen fat-free whipped topping, thawed
  3 tablespoons chopped hazelnuts, toasted

1. Place first 6 ingredients in a food processor; process 20 seconds or until smooth.
2. Place chocolate chips in a small microwave-safe bowl. Microwave at HIGH 1 minute; stir until smooth. Add chocolate to tofu mixture; process until smooth. Transfer mousse to a bowl; cover and chill at least 2 hours.
3. Spoon about ⅓ cup mousse into each of 9 small dishes. Coarsely crush 2 graham crackers over each mousse cup. Top each mousse cup with 1 tablespoon fat-free whipped topping, and sprinkle with 1 teaspoon hazelnuts. **Yield:** 9 servings (serving size: 1 mousse cup).

Per serving: CALORIES 142 (27% from fat); FAT 4.2g (saturated fat 1.5g); PROTEIN 5.7g; CARBOHYDRATES 20.1g; FIBER 1.9g; CHOLESTEROL 0mg; IRON 1.3mg; SODIUM 88mg; CALCIUM 26mg

Mandarin Oranges with Grand Marnier and Mascarpone

prep: 8 minutes

POINTS value: 5

Mascarpone's silky thick texture adds body and creaminess to the sour cream mixture. If you like, you can make a close substitute by using regular cream cheese.

¼	cup reduced-fat sour cream
2	tablespoons mascarpone cheese
4	teaspoons sugar
1	(15-ounce) can mandarin oranges in light syrup, drained
1½	tablespoons Grand Marnier (orange-flavored liqueur) or orange juice
	Mint leaves (optional)

1. Combine first 3 ingredients in a small bowl, stirring with a whisk until sugar completely dissolves.

2. Combine oranges and liqueur; spoon evenly into 3 wine glasses or dessert dishes. Spoon sour cream mixture over oranges; garnish with mint leaves, if desired. **Yield:** 3 servings (serving size: about 2½ tablespoons oranges and 1 tablespoon sour cream topping).

Per serving: CALORIES 200 (50% from fat); FAT 11g (saturated fat 6.2g); PROTEIN 3g; CARBOHYDRATES 19.9g; FIBER 0.8g; CHOLESTEROL 34mg; IRON 0.3mg; SODIUM 28mg; CALCIUM 72mg

Cream Cheese Baklava Cups

prep: 6 minutes • **cook:** 5 minutes

POINTS value: 1

These creamy treats are great for entertaining. If you don't want to serve all of them at once, keep the sour cream mixture stored in the refrigerator for up to 2 days, and assemble the cups as desired.

- 1 (2.1-ounce) package mini phyllo shells (such as Athens)
- ⅓ cup reduced-fat sour cream
- 2 tablespoons ⅓-less-fat cream cheese, softened
- 2 tablespoons light brown sugar
- 1 teaspoon vanilla extract
- ¼ cup chopped walnuts, toasted
- 2 tablespoons honey

1. Preheat oven to 350°.

2. Toast phyllo shells at 350° for 5 minutes. Let cool slightly.

3. While phyllo shells cook, combine sour cream and next 3 ingredients in a small bowl; beat with a mixer at medium speed until smooth. Fill phyllo shells evenly with sour cream mixture. Top with chopped walnuts and drizzle with honey.

Yield: 15 servings (serving size: 1 baklava cup).

Per serving: CALORIES 61 (50% from fat); FAT 3.4g (saturated fat 0.8g); PROTEIN 0.9g; CARBOHYDRATES 6.8g; FIBER 0.1g; CHOLESTEROL 3mg; IRON 0.3mg; SODIUM 24mg; CALCIUM 12mg

Apple Pie Scoops

prep: 5 minutes • **cook:** 13 minutes

POINTS value: 6

This dessert is essentially a deconstructed applesauce pie. Cooking the "filling" separately from the crust shaves off loads of time. Scoop up the applesauce with the crisp, spice strips.

½ (15-ounce) refrigerated pie dough (such as Pillsbury)
Butter-flavored cooking spray
4 teaspoons bottled cinnamon-sugar, divided
1 (24-ounce) jar chunky applesauce (such as Musselman's)
1 tablespoon brown sugar
2 teaspoons butter
6 tablespoons vanilla fat-free ice cream (such as Edy's)

1. Preheat oven to 425°.
2. Line a large baking sheet with parchment paper. Roll pie dough to a 12-inch circle on a lightly floured surface. Pierce entire surface liberally with a fork. With a pastry wheel or sharp knife, cut dough into 3 x 1–inch strips. Place strips on pan lined with parchment paper. Lightly coat strips with cooking spray; sprinkle evenly with 2 teaspoons cinnamon-sugar. Bake at 425° for 13 minutes or until golden brown.
3. While dough strips bake, combine applesauce, remaining 2 teaspoons cinnamon-sugar, brown sugar, and butter in a medium saucepan. Place over medium heat; cook 6 minutes or until sugars dissolve, stirring occasionally.
4. Spoon applesauce mixture into each of 6 serving dishes. Top each serving with 1 tablespoon ice cream, if desired, and serve with cinnamon strips. **Yield:** 6 servings (serving size: about ½ cup applesauce mixture and 8 cinnamon strips).

Per serving: CALORIES 283 (34% from fat); FAT 10.8g (saturated fat 4.1g); PROTEIN 1.3g; CARBOHYDRATES 46.1g; FIBER 1.4g; CHOLESTEROL 7mg; IRON 0.4mg; SODIUM 192mg; CALCIUM 17mg

Warm Apricots with Greek Yogurt and Walnuts

prep: 1 minute • **cook:** 14 minutes

POINTS value: 3

Enjoy this recipe now with dried apricots, and again when fresh apricots are in season. Simply combine the orange juice and ginger, and cook until the mixture is reduced to a syrup. Then stir halved fresh apricots into the warm orange syrup, and proceed as directed in the recipe.

16 dried apricots (about 4 ounces)
1 cup orange juice
1 teaspoon grated peeled fresh ginger
1 cup vanilla low-fat Greek yogurt (such as Oikos)
2 teaspoons honey
2 tablespoons chopped walnuts, toasted

1. Combine first 3 ingredients in a small skillet; bring to a boil over high heat. Cook 12 minutes or until apricots are plump and liquid is syrupy and reduced to about 1 tablespoon.

2. While apricots cook, spoon ¼ cup yogurt into each of 4 small bowls. Remove apricots from syrup, and divide evenly among bowls; drizzle apricots in each bowl with about 1 teaspoon syrup and ½ teaspoon honey. Sprinkle each serving with 1½ teaspoons walnuts. **Yield:** 4 servings (serving size: 4 apricots, ¼ cup yogurt, ½ teaspoon honey, and 1½ teaspoons walnuts).

Per serving: CALORIES 175 (13% from fat); FAT 2.5g (saturated fat 0.2g); PROTEIN 7g; CARBOHYDRATES 30.9g; FIBER 1.7g; CHOLESTEROL 0mg; IRON 1.5mg; SODIUM 26mg; CALCIUM 95mg

Rum-Glazed Bananas with Bittersweet Chocolate Sauce

prep: 4 minutes • **cook:** 16 minutes

POINTS value: 5

This dessert is reminiscent of Bananas Foster, but we eliminated the flambé step and added cinnamon and chocolate sauce.

⅓ cup granulated sugar
⅓ cup evaporated fat-free milk
¼ cup Dutch process cocoa
¼ cup dark chocolate chips (such as Hershey's Special Dark)
1 teaspoon vanilla extract
1½ tablespoons butter
¼ cup dark rum
¼ cup packed brown sugar
½ teaspoon ground cinnamon
⅛ teaspoon salt
4 firm ripe bananas, peeled and halved lengthwise
4 cups vanilla fat-free ice cream (such as Edy's)

1. Combine first 3 ingredients in a small saucepan over medium-high heat; stir well with a whisk. Bring to a boil; cook 3 minutes, stirring constantly. Remove from heat; add chocolate chips and vanilla, stirring until smooth. Set aside.

2. Combine butter and next 4 ingredients in a large nonstick skillet over medium-high heat. Cook 3 minutes or until sugar melts, stirring frequently. Add bananas, and cook 3 minutes on each side or until soft.

3. To serve, scoop ½ cup ice cream into each of 8 dessert dishes. Divide banana mixture evenly among dishes, and drizzle with chocolate sauce. Serve immediately. **Yield:** 8 servings (serving size: ½ cup ice cream, ½ banana, and about 1½ tablespoons chocolate sauce).

Per serving: CALORIES 279 (18% from fat); FAT 5.6g (saturated fat 2.7g); PROTEIN 4.7g; CARBOHYDRATES 56.2g; FIBER 5.4g; CHOLESTEROL 6mg; IRON 0.7mg; SODIUM 119mg; CALCIUM 142mg

Berry-Pomegranate Sauce

prep: 4 minutes • **cook:** 8 minutes

POINTS value: 1

This versatile sauce can be served over angel food cake, fat-free ice cream, or frozen yogurt. A ½-cup serving of sauce over a 2-ounce slice of angel food cake has a POINTS value of 3.

  2 tablespoons sugar
  1 tablespoon cornstarch
  ¼ teaspoon ground cinnamon
  ½ cup pomegranate juice
  1 (16-ounce) package frozen unsweetened mixed berries

1. Combine first 3 ingredients in a large saucepan, stirring with a whisk. Add juice, stirring with a whisk until smooth. Stir in berries. Bring to a boil over medium-high heat; cook 2 minutes or until thick, stirring constantly. Remove from heat. Serve immediately, or cover and chill. **Yield:** 5 servings (serving size: ½ cup).

Per serving: CALORIES 85 (0% from fat); FAT 0g (saturated fat 0g); PROTEIN 0.8g; CARBOHYDRATES 20.5g; FIBER 2.7g; CHOLESTEROL 0mg; IRON 0.5mg; SODIUM 3mg; CALCIUM 18mg

Chocolate-Mint Pudding Cups

prep: 5 minutes • **other:** 5 minutes

POINTS value: 2

Chocolate and mint create a perfect marriage of flavors in this easy-to-assemble dessert.

  2 cups fat-free milk
  ⅛ teaspoon peppermint extract
  1 (1.4-ounce) package sugar-free chocolate instant pudding mix
  ¼ cup frozen fat-free whipped topping, thawed
  4 crème de menthe chocolaty mint thins, chopped (such as Andes Mints)
Fresh mint sprigs (optional)

1. Combine milk and extract in a medium bowl, stirring with a whisk. Add pudding mix, stirring with a whisk until smooth.

2. Pour ½ cup pudding into each of 4 (6-ounce) ramekins or custard cups. Cover and refrigerate 5 minutes.

3. Spoon 1 tablespoon whipped topping onto each serving; top evenly with chopped candy. Garnish with mint sprigs, if desired. **Yield:** 4 servings (serving size: 1 pudding cup).

Per serving: CALORIES 109 (13% from fat); FAT 1.6g (saturated fat 1.4g); PROTEIN 5.7g; CARBOHYDRATES 18g; FIBER 0g; CHOLESTEROL 3mg; IRON 0.7mg; SODIUM 350mg; CALCIUM 150mg

Skillet Cherry-Pear Pie

prep: 4 minutes • **cook:** 10 minutes

POINTS value: 5

While the filling cooks on the stovetop, bake the crust in the oven so you can enjoy this comforting dessert in record time. Top each serving with ½ cup vanilla fat-free ice cream for an additional *POINTS* value of 1. Save time by using a refrigerated piecrust instead of a piecrust made from scratch.

- ½ (15-ounce) package refrigerated pie dough (such as Pillsbury)
- Cooking spray
- ½ cup sugar, divided
- ¼ teaspoon ground cinnamon
- 2 (14.5-ounce) cans pitted tart red cherries in water, undrained
- 1 tablespoon cornstarch
- 2 very ripe Bartlett or Anjou pears, peeled, cored, and chopped
- ⅛ teaspoon almond extract

1. Preheat oven to 450°.

2. Unroll dough onto a large baking sheet coated with cooking spray; pierce dough with a fork. Lightly coat dough with cooking spray. Combine 1 tablespoon sugar and cinnamon in a small bowl, stirring well; sprinkle over dough. Bake at 450° for 10 minutes or until golden and crisp.

3. While crust bakes, drain cherries, reserving ⅓ cup juice. Combine remaining 7 tablespoons sugar and cornstarch in a large nonstick skillet, stirring with a whisk. Add reserved juice, stirring with a whisk until smooth. Add cherries, pear, and almond extract. Bring to a boil over medium-high heat, stirring frequently. Cook 1 to 2 minutes or until thick, stirring constantly.

4. Carefully place crust on top of filling in pan; serve warm or at room temperature.

Yield: 8 servings (serving size: ⅛ of pie).

Per serving: CALORIES 223 (29% from fat); FAT 7.1g (saturated fat 2.5g); PROTEIN 2g; CARBOHYDRATES 40.8g; FIBER 2.6g; CHOLESTEROL 0mg; IRON 0.5mg; SODIUM 142mg; CALCIUM 18mg

pictured on page 126

Irish Cream Chocolate Pudding Cakes

prep: 9 minutes • **cook:** 11 minutes   ***POINTS*** value: 6

With rich chocolate flavor and a warm gooey filling, these hot-from-the-oven minicakes are the perfect indulgence at the end of a busy day.

- ⅔ cup all-purpose flour
- ¼ cup packed light brown sugar
- ¼ cup Dutch process cocoa, divided
- 1½ teaspoons baking powder
- ⅛ teaspoon salt
- ½ cup 1% low-fat milk
- 2 tablespoons light stick butter, melted
- 1 large egg, lightly beaten
- 1 teaspoon vanilla extract
- Cooking spray
- ⅓ cup packed light brown sugar
- ¾ cup hot water
- 2 tablespoons Irish cream liqueur (such as Bailey's)
- ½ cup vanilla fat-free ice cream (such as Edy's)

1. Preheat oven to 400°.

2. Lightly spoon flour into a dry measuring cup; level with a knife. Combine flour, ¼ cup brown sugar, 2 tablespoons cocoa, baking powder, and salt in a medium bowl. Combine milk and next 3 ingredients, stirring with a whisk. Add to dry ingredients, stirring just until moist. Spoon evenly into 4 (10-ounce) custard cups or ramekins coated with cooking spray.

3. Combine ⅓ cup brown sugar, remaining 2 tablespoons cocoa, ¾ cup hot water, and liqueur in a 2-cup glass measure. Microwave at HIGH 1 minute or until almost boiling; pour evenly over batter in custard cups.

4. Bake at 400° for 10 minutes or until almost set. Serve warm with ice cream.

Yield: 4 servings (serving size: 1 molten cake and 2 tablespoons ice cream).

Per serving: CALORIES 298 (22% from fat); FAT 7.2g (saturated fat 2.4g); PROTEIN 6g; CARBOHYDRATES 56.6g; FIBER 1.8g; CHOLESTEROL 62mg; IRON 2.5mg; SODIUM 310mg; CALCIUM 225mg

Caramel-Toffee Layered Dessert

prep: 12 minutes

POINTS value: 7

Sweet caramel plus crunchy toffee bits add up to a luscious layered dessert that requires no cooking.

   1   (10-ounce) loaf frozen reduced-fat pound cake (such as Sara Lee), thawed
   ⅔   cup Italian Sweet Crème coffee creamer (such as Nestlé Coffee-mate Liquid Italian Series), divided
   2   cups frozen fat-free whipped topping, thawed
   ⅓   cup fat-free caramel topping
   ½   cup toffee bits (such as Heath), divided

1. Cut pound cake lengthwise into 4 slices. Place 2 slices, cut sides up, in an 8-inch square baking dish. Brush tops with ⅛ cup coffee creamer.
2. Place whipped topping in a medium bowl; gently fold in caramel topping. Spread half whipped topping mixture over pound cake in baking dish. Sprinkle with ¼ cup toffee bits. Repeat layers with remaining pound cake, creamer, whipped topping mixture, and toffee bits. Cover and chill until ready to serve. Cut into 9 squares. **Yield:** 9 servings (serving size: 1 square).

Per serving: CALORIES 301 (33% from fat); FAT 11.1g (saturated fat 3.6g); PROTEIN 1.8g; CARBOHYDRATES 48.4g; FIBER 0g; CHOLESTEROL 0mg; IRON 0.1mg; SODIUM 272mg; CALCIUM 6mg

Ten-Minute Raisin Bread Pudding

prep: 4 minutes • **cook:** 6 minutes

POINTS value: 3

Substituting maple syrup for the bourbon and leaving the raisin bread whole makes great cinnamon-raisin French toast with a creamy maple sauce.

¼ cup egg substitute
2 tablespoons 1% low-fat milk
1 teaspoon vanilla extract
Cooking spray
4 (1-ounce) slices cinnamon-raisin swirl bread (such as Nature's Own)
¼ cup fat-free sweetened condensed milk
1 tablespoon bourbon

1. Combine first 3 ingredients in a shallow dish.

2. Place a griddle or a large nonstick skillet over medium heat until hot. Coat pan with cooking spray. Place bread slices in milk mixture, quickly turning to coat both sides. Cook 3 minutes on each side or until lightly browned. Remove from pan. Cut bread into 1-inch cubes; divide cubes evenly among 4 dessert dishes.

3. Combine sweetened condensed milk and bourbon; stir well. Drizzle bourbon sauce evenly over bread cubes. **Yield:** 4 servings (serving size: 1 bread slice and about 4 teaspoons bourbon sauce).

Per serving: CALORIES 168 (9% from fat); FAT 1.6g (saturated fat 0.7g); PROTEIN 6.2g; CARBOHYDRATES 29g; FIBER 1g; CHOLESTEROL 3mg; IRON 1.2mg; SODIUM 156mg; CALCIUM 217mg

Zabaglione with Fresh Berries

prep: 3 minutes • **cook:** 7 minutes

POINTS value: 4

We've reduced some of the fat and calories of traditional zabaglione—a light Italian custard made with egg yolks, sugar, and Marsala wine—by replacing some of the egg yolks with egg whites. Here we serve zabaglione hot when it's just made, but if you want to serve it chilled, refrigerate it up to an hour.

    2   large eggs
    2   large egg yolks
    ½   cup sugar
    ½   cup sweet Marsala wine
    3   cups whole mixed berries
    1½ cups light canned refrigerated whipped topping (such as Reddi-wip)

1. Combine first 4 ingredients in top of a double boiler, stirring with a whisk. Cook over simmering water, whisking constantly, about 7 minutes or until a thermometer registers 160°. Serve over berries. Top each serving with whipped topping. **Yield:** 6 servings (serving size: about ½ cup zabaglione, ½ cup berries, and ¼ cup whipped topping).

Per serving: CALORIES 200 (23% from fat); FAT 5g (saturated fat 2.8g); PROTEIN 3.6g; CARBOHYDRATES 32g; FIBER 1.8g; CHOLESTEROL 139mg; IRON 0.9mg; SODIUM 29mg; CALCIUM 32mg

Date-Walnut Gingersnap Sandwich Cookies

prep: 11 minutes • **cook:** 4 minutes

POINTS value: 2

If you don't plan to serve all the cookies at once, wrap them individually in plastic wrap, and store them at room temperature. The cookies will soften after a couple of hours and remind you of fig bars.

    1   large navel orange
    1½   cups chopped pitted dates
    ½   cup chopped walnuts
    ½   teaspoon ground cinnamon
    40   gingersnap cookies (such as Nabisco)

1. Grate ½ teaspoon rind and squeeze 6 tablespoons juice from orange. Combine orange rind, juice, dates, walnuts, and cinnamon in a medium saucepan. Cook over medium heat 4 minutes or until liquid almost evaporates and mixture is thick, stirring frequently. Let cool slightly.

2. Spoon about 1 tablespoon fruit mixture onto flat side of 20 cookies; top with remaining cookies (flat side to filling), and gently press until filling reaches edges.

Yield: 20 servings (serving size: 1 cookie sandwich).

Per serving: CALORIES 115 (26% from fat); FAT 3.3g (saturated fat 0.5g); PROTEIN 1.6g; CARBOHYDRATES 21.1g; FIBER 1.4g; CHOLESTEROL 0mg; IRON 1.1mg; SODIUM 92mg; CALCIUM 21mg

Peanut Butter Brownie Cookies

prep: 11 minutes • **cook:** 9 minutes   ***POINTS*** value: 1

These dense cookies don't spread much on the pan, so there is room for all of them in one batch. Natural peanut butter is the kind with a layer of oil on top, which needs to be stirred back into the peanut butter before using. Although it's not as creamy as regular peanut butter, it doesn't have trans fatty acids and is high in monounsaturated fat. Natural peanut butter has more flavor and works perfectly in these rich cookies.

  2⅓ cups low-fat fudge brownie mix (such as Betty Crocker)
   3 tablespoons natural-style chunky peanut butter
   2 tablespoons 1% low-fat milk
   2 tablespoons egg substitute
      Cooking spray
   2 tablespoons lightly salted, dry-roasted peanuts, chopped

1. Preheat oven to 375°.
2. Lightly spoon brownie mix into a dry measuring cup; level with a knife. Combine brownie mix, peanut butter, milk, and egg substitute in a large bowl. Drop by level tablespoonfuls about 1 inch apart onto a baking sheet coated with cooking spray. Sprinkle with peanuts, pressing peanuts gently into dough.
3. Bake at 375° for 9 minutes or until puffed. Remove cookies to wire racks.
Yield: 25 cookies (serving size: 1 cookie).

Per serving: CALORIES 65 (29% from fat); FAT 2.1g (saturated fat 0.4g); PROTEIN 1.1g; CARBOHYDRATES 10.8g; FIBER 0.5g; CHOLESTEROL 0mg; IRON 0.3mg; SODIUM 62mg; CALCIUM 2mg

pictured on page 125

Blonde Oatmeal Cookies

prep: 6 minutes • **cook:** 7 minutes • **other:** 5 minutes

POINTS value: 2

A light sprinkle of turbinado sugar adds sparkle to these freshly baked cookies.

  3 tablespoons butter, melted
  ¼ cup brown sugar blend (such as Splenda)
  1 large egg
  ⅔ cup uncooked quick-cooking oats
  ½ cup self-rising flour
  1 tablespoon turbinado sugar or granulated sugar

1. Preheat oven to 375°.
2. Combine first 3 ingredients in a medium bowl, stirring with a whisk until smooth. Stir in oats and flour.
3. Drop by level tablespoonfuls onto a baking sheet lined with parchment paper. Flatten slightly with dampened fingers; sprinkle with sugar. Bake at 375° for 7 minutes or until lightly browned. Transfer parchment paper to a wire rack, and let cool 5 minutes. **Yield:** 13 cookies (serving size: 1 cookie).

Per serving: CALORIES 68 (45% from fat); FAT 3.4g (saturated fat 1.8g); PROTEIN 1.6g; CARBOHYDRATES 7.7g; FIBER 0.6g; CHOLESTEROL 23mg; IRON 0.6mg; SODIUM 85mg; CALCIUM 22mg

Crispy Chocolate–Brown Rice Squares

prep: 9 minutes • **cook:** 3 minutes • **other:** 15 minutes   ***POINTS*** value: 2

No more sticky fingers while spreading these treats in the pan. Our wax-paper trick makes it fast, and you'll have no mess.

Cooking spray
- 2 tablespoons non-hydrogenated buttery spread (such as Smart Balance)
- 2½ cups miniature marshmallows (about 4 ounces)
- 2 tablespoons Dutch process cocoa
- 4 cups oven-toasted brown rice cereal (such as Erewhon)
- ¼ cup white chocolate chips or semisweet chocolate chips

1. Line bottom and sides of a 9-inch square baking pan with foil, allowing 2 to 3 inches to extend over sides; coat with cooking spray.

2. Combine buttery spread and marshmallows in a large microwave-safe bowl. Microwave at HIGH 1½ minutes. Add cocoa, stirring with a whisk. Stir in cereal; spoon into prepared pan. Cover with wax paper, and press down firmly to spread cereal mixture to edges of pan; discard wax paper.

3. Place white chocolate chips in a small heavy-duty zip-top plastic bag. Do not seal bag. Microwave at HIGH 45 seconds or until melted. Snip off 1 tiny corner of bag; squeeze bag to drizzle chocolate over cereal mixture in pan. Chill 15 minutes or until chocolate is set. Use foil edges to lift and remove cereal mixture from pan. Cut into squares. **Yield:** 16 servings (serving size: 1 square).

Per serving: CALORIES 78 (24% from fat); FAT 2.1g (saturated fat 0.8g); PROTEIN 0.9g; CARBOHYDRATES 15g; FIBER 0.7g; CHOLESTEROL 1mg; IRON 0.2mg; SODIUM 21mg; CALCIUM 8mg

Fruit-and-Nut Crispy Bars

prep: 6 minutes • **cook:** 2 minutes

POINTS value: 4

These bars are similar to date-nut balls and can be whipped up in less than 10 minutes.

  Butter-flavored cooking spray
  1 (10-ounce) package large marshmallows
  1½ tablespoons light stick butter
  7 cups chocolate-flavored oven-toasted rice cereal (such as Cocoa Krispies)
  1 (7-ounce) package dried fruit bits (such as Sun-Maid)
  ½ cup chopped pitted dates
  ⅓ cup chopped pecans

1. Coat a 13 x 9–inch baking pan with cooking spray.
2. Combine marshmallows and butter in a large microwave-safe bowl. Microwave at HIGH 2 minutes. Stir quickly until smooth. Quickly stir in cereal and remaining ingredients. Spoon into prepared pan. Cover with wax paper, and press down firmly to spread cereal mixture to edges of pan. Discard wax paper. Cut into 18 bars. **Yield:** 18 servings (serving size: 1 bar).

Per serving: CALORIES 185 (13% from fat); FAT 2.7g (saturated fat 0.9g); PROTEIN 1.8g; CARBOHYDRATES 40g; FIBER 1.1g; CHOLESTEROL 1mg; IRON 3.8mg; SODIUM 145mg; CALCIUM 13mg

Chocolate Cracker Bark

prep: 6 minutes • **cook:** 2 minutes • **other:** 10 minutes   *POINTS* value: 3

Chocolate lovers will be delighted with these decadent chocolate-covered crackers. Almonds and apricots add the perfect crunch and flavor to this quick pick-up dessert you will want to make again and again. Matzo is an unleavened bread, made of flour and water, that is traditionally served during the Jewish Passover holiday. You can find matzo in the international section of your grocery store.

2 (1-ounce) unsalted matzo crackers (such as Streit's)
1 (4-ounce) bar bittersweet chocolate (such as Ghirardelli), chopped
2 tablespoons chopped almonds, toasted
2 tablespoons finely chopped dried apricots

1. Arrange crackers on a rimmed baking sheet lined with parchment or wax paper.
2. Place chocolate in a microwave-safe bowl; microwave at HIGH 1 minute. Stir chocolate, and microwave an additional 30 seconds. Pour chocolate over crackers, spreading until crackers are covered. Sprinkle evenly with almonds and apricots, pressing into chocolate; let stand 10 minutes until hardened. Cut into 8 pieces.
Yield: 8 servings (serving size: 1 piece).

Per serving: CALORIES 113 (54% from fat); FAT 6.8g (saturated fat 3.1g); PROTEIN 2.2g; CARBOHYDRATES 15.1g; FIBER 1.6g; CHOLESTEROL 0mg; IRON 0.7mg; SODIUM 0mg; CALCIUM 5mg

Index

10 Simple Side Dishes

Vegetable	Servings	Preparation	Cooking Instructions
Asparagus	3 to 4 per pound	Snap off tough ends. Remove scales, if desired.	To steam: Cook, covered, on a rack above boiling water 2 to 3 minutes. To boil: Cook, covered, in a small amount of boiling water 2 to 3 minutes or until crisp-tender.
Broccoli	3 to 4 per pound	Remove outer leaves and tough ends of lower stalks. Wash; cut into spears.	To steam: Cook, covered, on a rack above boiling water 5 to 7 minutes or until crisp-tender.
Carrots	4 per pound	Scrape; remove ends, and rinse. Leave tiny carrots whole; slice large carrots.	To steam: Cook, covered, on a rack above boiling water 8 to 10 minutes or until crisp-tender. To boil: Cook, covered, in a small amount of boiling water 8 to 10 minutes or until crisp-tender.
Cauliflower	4 per medium head	Remove outer leaves and stalk. Wash. Break into florets.	To steam: Cook, covered, on a rack above boiling water 5 to 7 minutes or until crisp-tender.
Corn	4 per 4 large ears	Remove husks and silks. Leave corn on the cob, or cut off kernels.	Cook, covered, in boiling water to cover 8 to 10 minutes (on cob) or in a small amount of boiling water 4 to 6 minutes (kernels).
Green beans	4 per pound	Wash; trim ends, and remove strings. Cut into 1½-inch pieces.	To steam: Cook, covered, on a rack above boiling water 5 to 7 minutes. To boil: Cook, covered, in a small amount of boiling water 5 to 7 minutes or until crisp-tender.
Potatoes	3 to 4 per pound	Scrub; peel, if desired. Leave whole, slice, or cut into chunks.	To boil: Cook, covered, in boiling water to cover 30 to 40 minutes (whole) or 15 to 20 minutes (slices or chunks). To bake: Bake at 400° for 1 hour or until done.
Snow peas	4 per pound	Wash; trim ends, and remove tough strings.	To steam: Cook, covered, on a rack above boiling water 2 to 3 minutes. Or sauté in cooking spray or 1 teaspoon oil over medium-high heat 3 to 4 minutes or until crisp-tender.
Squash, summer	3 to 4 per pound	Wash; trim ends, and slice or chop.	To steam: Cook, covered, on a rack above boiling water 6 to 8 minutes. To boil: Cook, covered, in a small amount of boiling water 6 to 8 minutes or until crisp-tender.
Squash, winter (including acorn, butternut, and buttercup)	2 per pound	Rinse; cut in half, and remove all seeds. Leave in halves to bake, or peel and cube to boil.	To boil: Cook cubes, covered, in boiling water 20 to 25 minutes. To bake: Place halves, cut sides down, in a shallow baking dish; add ½ inch water. Bake, uncovered, at 375° for 30 minutes. Turn and season, or fill; bake an additional 20 to 30 minutes or until tender.